WEAPON

THE WEBLEY
SERVICE REVOLVER

ROBERT MAZE

Series Editor Martin Pegler

OSPREY PUBLISHING
Bloomsbury Publishing Plc

Kemp House, Chawley Park, Oxford OX2 9PH, UK
29 Earlsfort Terrace, Dublin 2, Ireland
1385 Broadway, 5th Floor, New York, NY 10018, USA
Email: info@ospreypublishing.com
www.ospreypublishing.com

OSPREY is a trademark of Osprey Publishing Ltd

First published in Great Britain in 2012

© Osprey Publishing Ltd, 2012

Transferred to digital print in 2024

A catalogue record for this book is available from the
British Library.

Print ISBN: 978 1 84908 803 9
ePDF: 978 1 84908 804 6
ePub: 978 1 78096 886 5

Page layout by Mark Holt
Index by Rob Munro
Battlescene artwork by Peter Dennis
Typeset in Sabon and Univers
Originated by PDQ Media, Bungay, UK
Printed and bound in India by Replika Press Private Ltd.

The Woodland Trust
Osprey Publishing supports the Woodland Trust, the UK's
leading woodland conservation charity.

www.ospreypublishing.com
To find out more about our authors and books visit our
website. Here you will find extracts, author interviews,
details of forthcoming events and the option to sign-up
for our newsletter.

Imperial War Museum Collections

Many of the photos in this book come from the Imperial War
Museum's huge collections which cover all aspects of conflict
involving Britain and the Commonwealth since the start of the
twentieth century. These rich resources are available online to
search, browse and buy at www.iwm.org.uk. In addition to
Collections Online, you can visit the Visitor Rooms where you
can explore over 8 million photographs, thousands of hours of
moving images, the largest sound archive of its kind in the world,
thousands of diaries and letters written by people in wartime,
and a huge reference library. To make an appointment, call:
(020) 7416 5320, or email: mail@iwm.org.uk

Imperial War Museum www.iwm.org.uk

Acknowledgments

Bob Maze would like to extend his warmest thanks to his wife
Laurie and the following cadre of like-minded folks; without
whose support, this book could not have been written:

Sgt B. Scott Berger, Samantha and John Denner,
Dr Robert Gussman, James Hallam, Capt Peter Laidler,
Molly and Richard Milner, Ian Patrick, 'The' Martin Pegler,
Joseph Salter Jr., Joseph Salter Sr., Robert Taylor, and the late
Maj David Thomas.

Peter Dennis would like to thank John Stallard of Warlord
Games for his generous loan of a Webley pistol for this project,
and for many other loans in the past from his collection.

Artist's note

Readers may care to note that the original paintings from which
the colour plates in this book were prepared are available for
private sale. All reproduction copyright whatsoever is retained by
the Publishers. All inquiries should be addressed to:

Peter Dennis, 'Fieldhead', The Park, Mansfield,
Nottinghamshire NG18 2AT, UK,
or email magie.h@ntlworld.com

The Publishers regret that they can enter into no correspondence
upon this matter.

Editor's note

For ease of comparison please refer to the following
conversion table:

1 mile = 1.6km
1yd = 0.9m
1ft = 0.3m
1in. = 2.54cm/25.4mm
1lb = 0.45kg

Image acknowledgements
Front cover images are courtesy of the Australian War Memorial
and the author's collection.

Title page image: Stanley Baker in *Zulu* wields a Mk VI Webley,
despite the fact that Rorke's Drift occured eight years before even
the Mk I was created. (Diamond Films/The Kobal Collection)

CONTENTS

INTRODUCTION

After Col Samuel Colt perfected the revolver's fundamental design in 1836, armies started to embrace the handgun as an effective means of close-quarters personal defence. By the last half of the 19th century, a trend emerged in the British Army – more military personnel were carrying revolvers. Until the *Dreadnought* era arrived in the 20th century, it was sailors who had most frequently carried pistols, because of their participation in boarding parties, but by the 1870s more land-based soldiers carried handguns. In the Army the pistol was no longer the exclusive domain of the officer. Non-commissioned officers (NCOs) and even wagon-drivers were now armed; the ability to defend oneself and to kill a lame or wounded horse mercifully were equally important.

'The Sun Never Sets on a Webley Revolver'; or so the engravings read on the last commercial .38in Webley revolvers sold before the closure of the great firm in the early 1980s. It may have been a marketing gimmick, but gimmick or not, the engraving bore out the truth. It hearkened back to an era when Britain's possessions covered the globe and the larger .455in ancestors of the little .38s were carried in the four corners of the Empire. While possibly not as overtly charismatic as the Colt Peacemaker, the Webley – specifically the various models of the hinge-frame .455in service revolver – had a working life and distribution far outstripping those of the Colt. It was carried as a useful tool both in conflict and in peacekeeping missions for more than 60 years, and in all of the areas of the globe to which British influence had extended. The large .455in revolver was immortal, too, on the silver screen, whenever the film industry required a 'typically British' revolver in the hand of a star acting out a passage from a period of history, even a period in which the Webley might never have existed.

From before the battle of Omdurman (1898) until after World War II, the Webley .455in revolver served British, Commonwealth and colonial soldiers, sailors, airmen, police officers and even African hunters well, when their lives depended on it most. This revolver progressed through six configurations, or 'marks' as the nomenclature reads. During this progression, it underwent a transformation that transcended the development of warfare, evolving as it was called upon to respond to ever-changing enemies and the tactics used to combat these new foes. Whether the fighting happened in a desert wadi or in the trenches of the Western Front, the Webley was present.

Conflict was not only restricted to the battlefield, but also existed in the back streets and gutters of cities, where police officers doing their day-to-day jobs wielded the Webley against vice and villainy. Curiously, the tactics of close-quarter fighting that developed in the depths of the trenches of World War I were taken up, recycled and refined by notable (ex-soldier) law-enforcement officers, like Eric Sykes and William Fairbairn of the Shanghai Municipal Police (SMP). Used in inter-war urban China to police the opium dens and gangster-strewn streets, these close-quarter fighting techniques carried through to World War II, when they were used for the training of elite Allied soldiers, such as the commandoes and airborne troops, and the agents of the British Special Operations Executive (SOE) and the American Office of Strategic Services (OSS). Now, more than 90 years on, modern-day elite Special Weapons and Tactics (SWAT) teams of police departments and elite military organizations around the world employ methods of personal defence and close-in combat that were developed initially for trench raiding in World War I, in which the Webley played a major role.

The .455in Webley service revolvers came into existence, as with most things of any significance, in a time of change. The change was in the way wars were being fought and in the engineering methods and capabilities of a country whose industrial revolution had hit its stride. After the American Civil War (1861–65), the concept of linear warfare – employing lines of armed men standing to win the day or fleeing to lose it – was rapidly disappearing. For Britain in the latter half of the 19th century the thin red lines of Wellington's day and the Crimea gradually faded into a khaki-

Able Seaman Joe W. 'Ginger' Scotcher cleaning Mk VI revolvers (and a M1928A1 Thompson submachine gun) in the armoury on board a British destroyer at Rosyth during World War II. (Imperial War Museum A 8363)

covered mosaic of soldiers fighting against foes that were now less 'orthodox' in their methods than earlier European enemies – the indigenous peoples of the empire who didn't abide by previously established rules of war. Throughout this period and by the early 20th century, the tactics and weapons of industrialized nations had evolved to the point of being far too lethal, thus making the old-fashioned ways of combat far too costly. Yet, this lesson would not be fully appreciated until the flower of a generation had fallen during World War I.

Wars are known to be catalysts for the development of both *matériel* and society. Yet when conflict is coupled with the might of an industrial machine, as in the late Victorian era, the progression is much more rapid. The revolver was initially embraced by the British military in the mid-1850s, at the end of the muzzle-loading era. From then until the acceptance of the Mk I .455in Webley revolver in 1887, the War Department had approved no fewer than nine different patterns of revolvers by five different makers. For devices that fundamentally all do the same thing (a trigger is pulled at one end and a projectile is expelled from the other), there are numerous ways to proceed. The lathes and milling machines of the industrial age enabled the inventors to express their talents by exploring all manner of fanciful new ideas. By the mid-1860s, steel was replacing iron in the manufacture of firearms and, for all intents and purposes, muzzle-loading was a thing of the past. The metallic cartridge era had arrived.

In the mid-19th century – much like today – there were two fundamental revolver designs: single-action, or those that were fired by thumb-cocking the hammer and releasing it with a short, crisp pull of the trigger; and double-action, which combined the prior two functions in one long pull of the trigger. Early revolvers were designed to be loaded and have their cartridges ejected at a single point, through a gate at the base of the cylinder, singly and slowly, one by one. Later, more advanced designs with hinged frames or swing-out cylinders, exposed a greater portion of the breech, allowed for more rapid loading and unloading. Additionally, there were problems from black-powder fouling and inadvertent cylinder rotation, both of which would quickly render a defensive weapon utterly useless (see the 'Development' section below). It was a lethal learning curve and, until the acceptance of the Webley, revolvers produced by either private or government manufacturers for the War Department had never combined all of the features important for the survival of a serviceman. The Webley Mk I .455in revolver was as close to the perfect storm of invention and manufacture that the era would permit, amalgamating a double-action lockwork, rapid loading, simultaneous extraction and ejection of cases, secure cylinder bolts to counteract random rotation and a robustness that defied the build-up of powder fouling.

The first .455in Service Webley, the Mk I. As perfect as 19th-century design could make it. (Author)

DEVELOPMENT
Britain's modern revolver

THE FIRST REVOLVERS IN SERVICE: 'NON-INTERCHANGEABLES' AND 'INTERCHANGEABLES'

The story of the Webley service revolver has its beginnings in the 1850s. Although no Webleys were in British service use at the time, this was the decade when the British military first embraced the revolver as a useful tool of the soldier's profession. Revolving weapons have their roots as far back as the 17th century, but 'modern' revolvers truly originated in 1836 with Samuel Colt's novel design. Colt had streamlined and perfected the percussion muzzle-loading revolver, incorporating unique features such as recessed nipples that were in line with the chambers and a separate cylinder, instead of a rotating array of chambers and attached barrels as on 'pepperbox' revolvers. For many years his patents protected his design, but these safeguards expired in 1851, opening the field for competition. Until the middle of the 19th century, single-shot muzzle-loading pistols had been, when infrequently issued, the soldier's or sailor's only type of handgun. Then, at the time of the Crimean War (1854–56), the British Board of Ordnance (BO), which in 1855 became the War Department (WD), ordered 23,700 London-manufactured Colt Model 1851 .36in (84-bore[1]) and 2,300 Deane, Adams & Deane .45in (54-bore) percussion muzzle-loading revolvers. For that era, this was an enormous purchase of a relatively new type of arm. Thus, a precedent had been set, and revolvers had been made an irrevocable part of the British military services. Despite this, there would be a long period of industrial change, innovation and

---

[1] The bore designation for a muzzle-loading weapon refers to the number of spherical projectiles of the weapon that would comprise 1lb in weight.

A typical English pepperbox pistol (*c.* 1840s) made by Mortimer, London. Note the revolving barrels and percussion nipples perpendicular to the line of the bore. Also note the complete lack of sights. Though advanced over the single-shot muzzle-loading pistol, it was not a weapon for the military. (Author)

The percussion revolver that made the transition in the British services to centre-fire: a War Department-marked Beaumont-Adams 54-bore (.45in) revolver. The facilities of both single- and double-action, and its heavy calibre, were attributes prized by its users and by the military. (Author)

experimentation in weapons' designs before the Webley entered service. These two early types of 'modern' service revolvers, the Colt and the Adams, were scarcely made from the same mould. The Colt Model 1851 was a small-bore single-action six-shot weapon, mass-produced and precision-made on the latest machinery. The Adams was a large-bore (and initially) double-action-only five-shot pistol, and although also machine-made, it was manufactured at a small London factory producing sporting arms for the British gun trade. Samuel Colt had introduced his products to Britain at the Great Exhibition of 1851. For a few years afterwards, his firearms became exceedingly popular, so much so that Colt built a large, modern factory in London to produce them.[2] Robert Adams invented his revolver while working as a partner of George and John Deane; its design had been in existence since 1851, and was also introduced to the public at the Great Exhibition. It had, by the time the WD purchased Adams' revolvers, been refined in 1854 from its original configuration, with a modification to the lockwork by Lt F.B.E. Beaumont RE (Royal Engineers), which allowed thumb- as well as trigger-cocking, i.e. both single and double-action firing.

In the peace that followed the Crimean conflict, the WD found itself with large stocks of incongruous forms of handguns, both single-shot pistols and revolvers, and was initially at a loss as to what to do with them. Not only did the military possess the Colt and the Adams, but also large stocks of the Enfield Pattern 1856 rifled single-shot .577in (25-bore) pistols that had traditionally been issued to cavalry sergeants. These pistols were an anachronism by the mid-19th century. Hard-hitting weapons that fired repeatedly with every double-action pull of the trigger were to become the order of the day. This trend also indirectly brought about the demise of

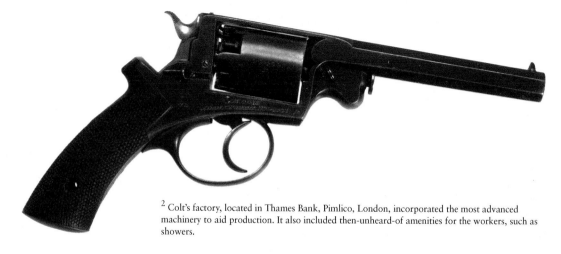

[2] Colt's factory, located in Thames Bank, Pimlico, London, incorporated the most advanced machinery to aid production. It also included then-unheard-of amenities for the workers, such as showers.

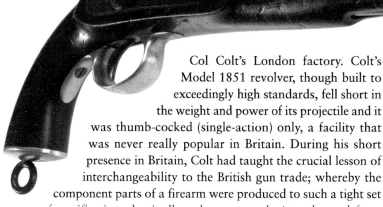

Col Colt's London factory. Colt's Model 1851 revolver, though built to exceedingly high standards, fell short in the weight and power of its projectile and it was thumb-cocked (single-action) only, a facility that was never really popular in Britain. During his short presence in Britain, Colt had taught the crucial lesson of interchangeability to the British gun trade; whereby the component parts of a firearm were produced to such a tight set of specifications that it allowed any part to be *interchanged*, from one arm to another, without significant additional hand fitting. This lesson was well learned and facilitated the expansion of the gun trade in Britain by making firearms manufactured to closer tolerances actually more economical to produce due to reduced labour costs. But possibly most importantly, it intrigued the WD with the prospect of less expensive service weapons that were easier to repair in the field. Alas, the Model 1851 began falling out of favour and Colt was soon unable to compete commercially, closing his factory in 1856. However, the WD kept the Colt revolvers in stores until the 1870s, when many were relegated to colonial service.

As the muzzle-loading percussion era drew to a close, a plethora of revolver designs was proffered by the gun trade, one of which in particular should be mentioned, as it was briefly considered as a service weapon by the British military. In 1856, Robert Adams parted company with the Deanes and, along with his gun-making machinery, helped form the London Armoury Company (LAC), where he was a principal stockholder and manager for two years. The LAC was formed by a group of cutting-edge gun-makers, using advanced manufacturing methods to compete directly with government factories for valuable contracts. The former foreman from Deanes, James Kerr, also joined the LAC. In 1859, Kerr offered a 54-bore version of his revolver to the Ordnance Select Committee for evaluation at the Royal Manufactory (RM) in Enfield, north of London. Kerr's was a straightforward design of total practicality, incorporating a side-mounted musket-type lock arrangement that could easily be detached for cleaning; in modern parlance, a sideplate. During its military trials, Kerr's weapon was praised for its simplicity, but it was all too simple, with few truly novel features, and it was single-action, which probably damned his revolver from the outset. A few hundred Kerrs were sold to various militia units in Britain, but the vast majority of the revolvers went to the Confederate States of America.

The Pattern 1856 Enfield rifled .577in (25-bore) muzzle-loading pistol, as issued to Lancers, Yeomanry and troop sergeant-majors of cavalry regiments; a basic design little-changed in 200 years. A detachable butt stock was a feature on some Yeomanry variants; with this accessory attached, its leaf sights (to 300yds) may have been somewhat useful. (Author)

A 'non-interchangeable' five-shot Adams Mk I (c. 1869) in .450in Boxer. Originally manufactured by the London Armoury Company, this pistol started its life in the 1850s as a percussion revolver; after the additions of a new cylinder, loading gate and ejection rod, it still retains the lanyard hole in its grip, which was usually plugged at the time of the revolver's conversion to centre-fire. (Author)

Though initially bought in fewer numbers than the Colt, the Adams prevailed as the accepted pattern of service handgun. Adams revolvers were to remain in service as frontline weapons until the 1880s. Between 1856 and 1865 the WD purchased an additional 5,000 revolvers from the LAC. A decade after their initial purchase, the WD Adams revolvers of the 1850s were modified to accept the new .450in Boxer[3] centre-fire breech-loading cartridge. From 1869, 7,000 54-bore percussion Adams, then in service or stores, were converted to centre-fire (LoC[4] §1738 & §1739) and designated initially as the Mk I. (In 1872 many Mk Is were retrofitted with a strengthened hand (pawl) and operating spring and renamed the Mk IV (LoC §2450).) This conversion to breech-loading was performed by another Adams – John – who was supposedly Robert's cousin (Chamberlain and Taylerson 1976: 16). John Adams was an innovative gun-maker, and possibly a genius when it came to revolver design. He was eventually to supply the WD with two subsequent types of revolvers, so at one point there were three variants of Adams revolvers in service; one designed by Robert, and two designed by John.

By 1870 the industrialization of the British gun trade was in full swing. Commercial arms were made on the latest precision milling machines. Thus complete interchangeability between weapons parts was (nearly) attained, something that the military had aspired to ever since their first glimpse of it in America when visiting the Springfield, MA, arsenal in 1853. The 1850s revolvers of Robert Adams were produced on less precise machinery that involved more hand fitting, and were officially referred to as 'non-interchangeables'. However, John Adams' later offerings were manufactured to tighter standards, and were known as 'interchangeables' in the official nomenclature.

[3] Col Edward Mounier Boxer RA (Royal Artillery), working at the Royal Laboratories at Woolwich, was the inventor of the first successful centre-fire cartridge for both long-arms (e.g. Snider) and handguns. The .450in Boxer Mk I and Mk II had built-up cases with iron or brass rims respectively, attached by a rivet through the primer pocket. The Mk III round had a drawn brass case. The Mk I and Mk II were declared obsolete in 1894, and the Mk III in 1921.

[4] *List of Changes in British War Matériel and of Patterns of Military Stores (Which Have Been Approved and Sealed; With Instructions Relating Thereto)*. The LoC was a War Department publication from 1860. The author Ian Skennerton has published five volumes that encompass the period 1860–1926.

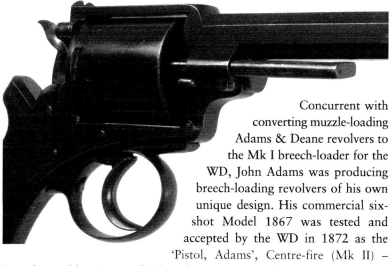

Concurrent with converting muzzle-loading Adams & Deane revolvers to the Mk I breech-loader for the WD, John Adams was producing breech-loading revolvers of his own unique design. His commercial six-shot Model 1867 was tested and accepted by the WD in 1872 as the 'Pistol, Adams', Centre-fire (Mk II) – Interchangeable'. Outwardly the Mk II was very similar to Robert Adams' converted (Mk I) revolver, with a loading gate and an ejector rod running parallel with the barrel. Subsequently, in 1873, the WD accepted another of John's designs as the Mk III (commercial Model 1872). The Mk III differed from its predecessor only in the configuration of the ejector rod, which on the Mk III nested within a cavity inside the cylinder arbour and pivoted into place when necessary. John's revolvers were modern enough for 1872, demonstrating the popular features of the day, but they, along with most other contemporary revolvers, were far from perfect.

THE IMPORTANCE OF PRIVATE PURCHASE

Traditionally, British officers at the time of their commissions bought a sidearm, or were presented with one by relatives, friends or their communities. These privately purchased commercial arms have irrevocable importance in the use and development of the British service revolver. From the 1850s until 1880, when the WD thought it could produce a revolver superior to those offered by the gun trade, privately purchased weapons came to be fielded far more frequently than government-issue revolvers. These serving officers with their privately purchased revolvers were a source of enlightenment. They were at the sharp end of battle, and discovered quickly which of the multitude of revolver or pistol designs worked as they were meant to, and which were no better than clubs, when the going got tough.

There were inherent problems in revolver design and also with the new Boxer centre-fire cartridges they used. The ability to load, eject spent cases, or unload a weapon quickly was bottlenecked by the simultaneous manipulations of a loading gate, an ejector rod and a cylinder. Another problem was that revolver cylinders of that era, when only partially loaded, had a troublesome tendency for the heavier loaded chambers to rotate towards the base of the frame, which could provide a shooter with an empty

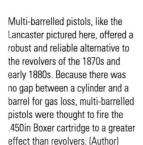

Multi-barrelled pistols, like the Lancaster pictured here, offered a robust and reliable alternative to the revolvers of the 1870s and early 1880s. Because there was no gap between a cylinder and a barrel for gas loss, multi-barrelled pistols were thought to fire the .450in Boxer cartridge to a greater effect than revolvers. (Author)

chamber at a critical moment. As an expedient to counter this problem, ejector rods were partially inserted into the fronts of chambers, and spring-powered friction brakes were also trialled, but these options were neither convenient nor totally effective. Black-powder fouling was also an unavoidable problem; its caking and corrosive effects had the ability to cause enough drag to stop cylinders from rotating and to jam cartridge cases solidly inside their chambers. Though Boxer's ammunition design was novel and convenient for that period, it depended on a built-up, or composite, cartridge whereby the rim disc of iron (Mk I) or brass (Mk II), as a separate piece, was riveted to the case through the primer pocket. No matter how well manufactured these cartridges were, faults occurred; cases split at their seams, rims detached themselves and primers blew out, jamming the cylinder against the recoil shield – not a very satisfactory situation in the heat of battle. And, though the .450in Boxer round had as its projectile a substantial piece of lead (225 grains), by the early 1880s the quantity of black powder that propelled it was thought by some to be slightly inadequate, this view being reinforced by reports from the Zulu and Afghan campaigns of 1878–81. However, given the highly innovative and exceedingly competitive nature of the gun trade of that period, solutions to these troubles were quickly attempted and incorporated into the flow of new handgun designs entering the marketplace.

One strategy used to remedy the failings of the revolver (and its ammunition) was the introduction of multi-barrelled pistols, which came in two basic varieties. The first form includes examples of two-barrel (over-and-under) and four-barrel break-open pistol-calibre weapons made by Charles Lancaster, Braendlin Armoury and Thomas Bland. These arms had no cylinders to jam, but were fired by a rotating striker that cycled sequentially between the chambers with every pull of the trigger. When broken open they extracted and ejected empty cases in the same forceful manner as a shotgun, and since there wasn't a gap between cylinder and barrel for gas to escape through, multi-barrelled weapons of this design improved the efficiency of the cartridge. This type of pistol proved very popular and reliable during a time when the virtues of a revolver were in some doubt, and then for quite a time after the revolver's limitations had been overcome.

The second of the multi-barrelled types was the two-barrel side-by-side large-bore pistol built on a modified sidelock sporting gun action.

These monstrosities, often chambered for a shortened version of the .577in Snider rifle cartridge, were commonly referred to as 'howdah pistols' after the weapons carried by tiger hunters in India riding in wicker baskets (howdahs) atop elephants. Howdah pistols were originally used as a last-ditch defence against attack by a large, wounded and ferocious feline, but for a time in the latter part of the 19th century were often carried through private purchase. While howdah pistols chambered far fewer rounds than revolvers, their stopping power was never in question.

Whether as a result of empirical evidence, mess hall gossip or marketing ploys by the trade, a few revolver models, also thought to be more powerful, were privately purchased. Most common were Colt models of 1873 and 1878 imported from America, chambered for the .45in long (Colt) cartridge. By the early 1880s, P. Webley & Sons was offering its No. 5 Army Express revolver also chambered for the .45in long Colt and, for whatever reason, this revolver bore an uncanny resemblance to the Colt Model 1878. Other, more home-grown varieties of potent pistols were supplied for private purchase by the trade as well. For example, the famous Birmingham gun-maker William Tranter offered five- and six-shot revolvers chambering the short, but powerful, .577in Boxer round. Though this calibre was assembled with the typical Boxer built-up case, Tranter's revolver design guarded against the inherent possibility of blown-out primers jamming the action with a breech plate the diameter of the cylinder. This plate, when in place, only allowed access for the hammer nose to penetrate and strike the cartridge primer.

THE WAR DEPARTMENT'S QUANDARY AND THE ENFIELD REVOLVERS

Throughout the 1870s those 'Little Wars' that today we associate with the reign of Queen Victoria were occurring with increasing frequency. In Egypt, in West and South Africa, and on the North-West Frontier in India, more troops were being mobilized and deployed and thus more weapons were needed. John Adams' small factory at 391 Strand, London, could not keep up with the increasing demand for pistols. So the WD made attempts to supplement its dwindling stocks of Adams revolvers with other arms, again, supplied by the trade. In July 1878, the WD purchased 2,000 revolvers from William Tranter; these revolvers were chambered for the .450in service cartridge and deemed 'interchangeable'. Unfortunately for the WD, the interchangeable Tranters were not uniformly able to accept the Boxer cartridge, the revolvers' tolerances being too tight and the manufacturing tolerances for the ammunition too loose, so these pistols were quickly withdrawn to be ultimately sold out of service. Nearly a year later, following the crushing early defeats of British forces in Natal by Zulu warriors, Tranter was again called upon to provide trade pattern 'non-interchangeable' 1867 models to the WD. Colt's London agency was approached to do the same in that time of crisis, providing 165 Model

A .450 Boxer revolver round compared to the short .577 'Howdah' and the full-length Boxer Snider rifle cartridges. (Author)

13

1878 'non-interchangeable' revolvers. Both the Tranter and the Colt commercial types purchased for the Zululand conflict were chambered for the .450in Boxer cartridge.

Up to 1880 all breech-loading service revolvers used by the British military had been gate-loaded, rod-ejecting types. This cumbersome form of pistol was rapidly losing the Victorian arms race to new models that would self-extract and simultaneously eject their spent cartridges. Since the mid-1870s a dissatisfaction had been growing in the military with its handguns. By 1879 the WD was at its wit's end over the ongoing shortage of revolvers, and over the various types of revolvers then in service with assorted manufacturing standards. With that situation at hand, the WD was bound and determined to set a new standard for the military with an interchangeable, self-extracting and 'modern' revolver. Yet what ultimately occurred was the development and adoption of a weapon that was created with the best intentions, but not necessarily the most practical ideas. This resulting arm, the amalgamation by the WD of Victorian arms technologies, was the Enfield Mk I revolver of 1880.

Though the ultimate design of the Enfield is commonly attributed to a Welsh-born American, Owen Jones, the revolver's lock components were a blending of existing configurations invented by gun-makers M. Jean Warnant, Michael Kaufmann and John Stanton (Taylerson 1966: 69–71). Owen Jones' contribution was the extraction system, which wasn't actually self- or simultaneously-extracting, but in fact, selectively extracting. When the hinge-framed pistol was broken open, all cases would be extracted from their chambers as the cylinder, staying in line with the frame, was pulled forward. This action allowed the spent cases to fall free, except for the one at the six o'clock position next to the frame, which until the cylinder was rotated slightly could not be released. This idiosyncrasy – along with loosening at its hinge and barrel catch after only minimal use, the disadvantages of its being gate-loading, and having no effective means (cylinder bolts) to counter inadvertent cylinder rotation – all contributed to the Mk I's short service life. Trying to be fair, but summing up the general attitude of the time, Maj H.E.C. Kitchener (a Sandhurst instructor; not to be confused with the famous field marshal) commented in 1886 on the Enfield that '[though] the pull-off is good, the weapon appears to me inaccurate and clumsy' (Taylerson 1966: 73).

The subsequent Enfield Mk II revolver, introduced in 1881, was a somewhat revamped version of its predecessor, incorporating a feeble

An Anglo-Zulu War-era Tranter 'non-interchangeable' (Commercial Model 1867). An emergency purchase, this revolver bears its legacy of service on its frame; marked with 'CSA' for the commercial purveyor, '3.79' for its date of acceptance into service, the War Department's 'WD' and broad arrow, and finally the opposed broad arrows denoting its eventual sale out of service. Also to be noted is a feeble attempt to retard inadvertent cylinder rotation in the form of a small friction spring just ahead of the cylinder. (Author)

attempt at a cylinder bolt in the form of a small tooth protruding at the base of the recoil shield. But it and the earlier Mk I shared yet another very serious Achilles heel. Initially, both marks of Enfield revolvers utilized a rebounding hammer as a safety feature to keep the hammer nose away from the cartridge primers. Unfortunately, the lock spring that powered the rebound mechanism was easily defeated by a sharp blow. This physical phenomenon was discovered in November 1886 much to the detriment of Lt Rooper RN, of HMS *Flying Fish*, when his Enfield fell to the deck of a longboat, discharged and he was shot cleanly through the head (Chamberlain & Taylerson 1989: 15). From 1887 until the early 1890s, when the Enfields were withdrawn completely from active service, they were re-fitted with one of two types of hammer-blocking safeties, very similar to those later used effectively in Smith & Wesson (S&W) revolvers. Many Enfield revolvers that found their way into colonial service in Canada until 1910, with the Northwest Mounted Police (from 1904 the Royal Northwest Mounted Police, and from 1920 the Royal Canadian Mounted Police), and in Australian and Indian police forces, were never retrofitted with these safety devices.

By the mid-1880s complaints about the Enfields emerged. Detractors said that they were too heavy to shoot accurately, too awkward to load easily, and generally too complicated for the uninitiated soldier to learn to use quickly. By 1886, personnel from all ranks seemed to be displeased with the Enfields. One person who was devastatingly instrumental in replacing the Enfields was the Army's adjutant-general, Sir Garnet Wolseley. He was a national hero, one of the Army's 'best and brightest', and his opinions were virtually dogma. When something was accomplished with great integrity, it was popularly said to be: 'All Sir Garnet'. He was after all, as Gilbert and Sullivan portrayed him in their operetta *The Pirates of Penzance*, 'the very model of a modern major general'. The time was ripe for change, and rigorous trials to find a new

The Enfield Mk I and Mk II revolvers. The Mk II exhibited a simplification in grip attachment and an inadequate attempt, in the form of a tooth protruding from the recoil shield, to stop undue cylinder rotation. (Author)

The problem with the Enfield's selective extraction – a spent case caught at the six o'clock position. (Author)

service revolver began in earnest at Enfield in the autumn of 1886, paving the way for the Webley.

Coming out of the rather stormy career of the Enfield was one silver lining that gleamed as an advancement for the revolver in British service – the discarding of the Boxer composite cartridge design in 1881 in favour of cartridges utilizing the more robust drawn-brass case. While the Enfield revolver was in active use, three marks of ammunition were approved for it, with the third mark persisting in service for a number of years thereafter. The rounds for the Enfield had larger case capacities than that of the Boxer and thus were more powerful, and, being seamless, they had less of a chance of coming apart and jamming the action. All of the bullets used by the three marks of cartridges weighed 265 grains, were made of a lead/tin (12:1) alloy, and had expanding bases. The Mk I and II cartridges used a .455in bullet seated into the case mouth in the standard manner, whereas the Mk III round was fitted with a .476in heel-based bullet.[5] The commercial Mk III cartridge was referred to in Eley or Kynoch ammunition catalogues of the day as the '.476', and persisted in availability until after World War I. Possibly due to the preponderance or popularity of this chambering from its introduction in 1881 onwards, Enfield revolvers were often colloquially referred to in terms of the .476in chambering.

[5] A heel-based bullet's widest diameter is that of the case, with a narrower portion, 'the heel', being inserted into the case mouth.

ENTER P. WEBLEY & SONS

The firm that was eventually to produce the .455in service revolver was Philip Webley (& Son). The company had its origins in the 1830s as a member of the Birmingham gun trade. By the mid-1830s, Philip and his elder brother James had completed their apprenticeships in the trade and were then fledgling gun-makers, initially producing only components (e.g. locks, barrels, etc.) for weapons. Philip, younger by six years, worked as a filer for his brother until 1838, then set out to find his own fortune in the trade. That same year he married Caroline, the daughter of a successful firearms accoutrement maker, William Davis. The next year when William passed away, Philip was able to take over his thriving business as the 'Successor to the Late William Davis – Manufacturers to the Honourable East India Company'.

Through the 1840s, Philip's business and family grew, and by 1851 his firm was manufacturing complete single-shot pistols, shotguns, and rifles. His two sons, Thomas William and Henry, would eventually follow successfully in their father's footsteps as capable gun-makers in their own right. Both James and Philip secured British patents in 1853 for revolver lock, frame and barrel construction. By 1855, both firms were producing revolvers of the most contemporary designs, on a par with both the Adams and Colt weapons of that period.

Following James' sudden death in 1856, Philip took over his brother's facilities and patents. Steady growth continued into the 1860s, with Webley embracing the breech-loading concept early on. In 1863 their factory was producing dubiously licensed copies of Colt's single-shot .41in rimfire derringer and S&W's tip-up rimfire revolver in .22 and .32 calibres. Webley's first big sale of arms to the government came in 1868, when the firm supplied the Royal Irish Constabulary (RIC) with 1,000 state-of-the-art solid-frame centre-fire revolvers in .442in. Subsequently, solid-frame constabulary-pattern revolvers were supplied to the London Metropolitan Police, and most other police organizations in Britain and the Commonwealth. By the mid-1870s, the British government was familiar with the weapons that Webley produced.

An early Webley .442in Royal Irish Constabulary Model revolver. (Author)

A refinement of the Kaufmann, the 'WG' (Webley Government) was the first Webley model to incorporate the robust stirrup-type barrel catch that would later be used on service models. (Author)

WEBLEY'S HINGE-FRAME REVOLVERS

Webley always seemed to have been interested in acquiring the means for producing weapons with novel features, to keep the company at the forefront of the highly competitive gun trade. Their first departure from the solid-frame type of revolver was in 1876 with the acquisition of Charles Pryse's British Patent 4421. The features pertaining to this patent dealt with cylinder locking bolts, and were incorporated in a self-extracting and ejecting hinge-frame pistol with a tong-type barrel catch. (Today these types of weapons are erroneously referred to as 'Pryse' revolvers.) From 1881 to 1885, Webley manufactured a sleek and finely finished hinge-frame under Michael Kaufmann's licence. This was the first glimpse of an arm with the visual and mechanical attributes that would shortly be incorporated in a service revolver.

The weak point of the Kaufmann design lay in its barrel catch, a push button/sliding bar arrangement that proved too fragile for extended service under the stresses of the more powerful ammunition that was just coming into use. Philip's son Henry and a colleague – John Carter – developed and patented (British Patent 4070/1885) a strong stirrup-type barrel catch and lock improvements for the Kaufmann. These improvements were assimilated into a new model of 'Improved Kaufmann', referred to as 'Webley's New Pattern Government Revolver', or simply 'WG'. This model was designed to catch the government's eye, and it did so, but it also became the weapon of choice for young officers starting their service careers, and for those who engaged in the increasingly popular sport of competitive target shooting. The WG was both durable and precise; it was a reliable sidearm to be carried into battle and, with a silky smooth action, an arm that was setting and repeatedly breaking its own records in the shooting galleries of Wimbledon.

Webley's Pistol, Revolver Mk I

Lord Wolseley vented his complaints of the Enfield revolver to the Surveyor of Ordnance on 8 July 1886. Also, after recommending his own weapon he sent it for consideration, describing it as a self-ejecting 'Bulldog'

type retailed by (Henry) Adams & Co. (Chamberlain & Taylerson 1989: 21). However, it is believed that Wolseley's revolver was actually a hinge-frame 'Pryse' type similar to the model sold by Webley, as their No. 4. Examples of this form of handgun, chambered for both Boxer and Enfield cartridges, were acquired from Adams & Co. and P. Webley & Sons for the initial reliability and accuracy trials at Enfield. Later a request originating from Enfield solicited Webley for the construction of a prototype. Strangely, this mock-up revolver, which has certain similarities in its action to the future accepted pattern, was a solid-frame rod-ejecting weapon (Milner 2008: 20; this particular revolver currently resides in the National Firearms Collection, Leeds, UK). The production of a more primitive design at this stage in the evolution of a state-of-the-art service weapon seems an incongruous step, so what part it played (lock or ammunition testing?) in the overall trials remains a mystery.

Finally, on 8 November 1887, the initial pattern was sealed for Webley's .442in[6] Mk I Service Revolver. The initial order, dating from 18 July 1887, from the Director of Army Contracts was for 10,000 units, with the final destination of these guns being the Navy. Much emphasis was placed by the WD on interchangeability, and Webley was given a certain degree of freedom in terms of time for when the first deliveries were to commence, as long as the firm could attain the elusive ideal of absolute interchangeability between component parts of their revolvers. Thus, it wasn't until January 1890 that Webley could guarantee weekly shipments of revolvers. The initial deliveries of 100 per week were soon increased to 150. Almost simultaneously, the original order for pistols was doubled (to 20,000), with 16,000 for the Navy and 4,000 for land service. With the inclusion of subsequent orders, more than 35,000 Mk I service revolvers had been produced by 1894.

The revolver itself was a solid hand-filling hinge-frame type that

The solid-frame revolver P. Webley & Son submitted to Enfield in 1887 ostensibly for ammunition testing. While its grip frame profile is similar to that of the future Mk I service weapon, the balance of its configuration is reminiscent of the earlier No. 5 Army Express. (© Royal Armouries)

[6] Until World War I (LoC §18980), most Webley revolvers were referred to not in terms of their ammunition, such as .455in, but instead in terms of their minimum gauged bore diameter measured with a cylindrical plug passed under the lands of the rifling. Initially, the trials and sealed patterns of Webley revolvers, as well as the early production guns, had a minimum bore diameter of .441in, though they fired a .455in (i.e. groove diameter) projectile.

offered an effective cylinder bolt and locking at two points when fired. It also had a tremendously positive mechanism for the simultaneous extraction and ejection of cartridges. The debilitating effects of black powder were overcome by a nearly frictionless bearing surface on which the cylinder could rotate, and a collar on the front of the cylinder, surrounding its axis, that overlapped a corresponding collar on the frame, thus forming a baffle to exclude fouling and corrosive gases.

The Mk I was the embodiment of perfected British 19th-century handgun manufacturing methods and design characteristics, which Webley had learned from sales to serving officers and target shooters alike. With a 4in barrel it was quick and true to point, and its bird's-head grip configuration fitted well into the hands of either the gauntleted cavalry trooper or the naval tar. Another intelligent amenity was the pair of triangular-shaped holster guides, mounted on either side of the barrel lug in front of the cylinder. These guides ensured that the cylinder wouldn't snag on the edge of the pistol case when the weapon was placed into it. This may seem as trivial to many, but maybe not to a Lancer on a galloping charger.

The designs of the action and major subassemblies of the Mk I came from both public and private sectors. Its particularly robust lockwork, containing only five major components, was modified from one invented by the Belgian C.F. Galand (British Patent 2308/1872). As a testament to the utility of the Galand type of action, which utilizes the mainspring to power both the hammer and pawl, it was further used by Webley in their commercial Mk II, III, and IV .320in and .380in handguns and by Colt in all of their double-action revolvers from 1889. Every previously mentioned feature unique to the Mk I, such as the extraction system, cylinder bolts, stirrup barrel catch, etc., was designed in-house and patented by Webley.

Simple and secure, a cross-screw type of cylinder retention/dismounting was used on Mk I (here), Mk I* and Mk II revolvers. (Author)

Early ammunition

With the supplanting of the .450in Boxer/Adams rounds (Mks I, II and III) in the 1880s, existing stocks of the old calibre were relegated to practice and emergency uses, as the .450in would chamber in all existing service pistols of the day. At the time of its adoption, the Webley service revolvers initially utilized the Enfield Mk II (.455in) and Mk III (.476in) cartridges with a 265-grain soft lead (a 12:1 lead:tin ratio) bullet then in use. It wasn't until 1891 that the Webley Mk I (.455in) black-powder round was adopted (LoC §6844). When the service cartridge did eventually change from Enfield to Webley, this shift was brought forth by technological advancement rather than from inherent problems with the Enfield loadings. The new Webley ammunition incorporated improvements in durability and in ignition. Black powder was used as a propellant for the Mk I cartridge until 1894, when a smokeless loading using the new nitrocellulose compound, cordite, was adopted. These early marks of Webley ammunition were finally declared obsolete in 1921.

The case length of these cartridges was 0.85–0.87in, the dimensions being determined by the burning characteristics of the black powder then in common use. Since their first practical use in small arms in 1884, smokeless powders were rapidly embraced by the world's militaries. Besides producing only a tiny amount of tell-tale smoke to betray a soldier's position, an equivalent amount of the new propellant could produce as much as three times the energy of black powder. By 1897, it was realized that by reducing

ABOVE

Left to right, a .450 Boxer in comparison with the Enfield Mk II and Mk III pistol cartridges. Commercially the Mk II round was referred to as the '.455' and the Mk III as the '.476' due to its wider heel-based bullet. (Author)

the case capacity (to a length of 0.74in–0.76in) more efficiency in combustibility and pressure could be attained with chopped cordite. Thus the Mk II round (LoC §9159) was born; its case dimensions and overall ballistic traits would carry this loading into the 20th century, and through two world wars. The Webley Mk I revolver, and all of the marks that followed, had long chambers in their cylinders that would accept any type of .455in round.

In the early marks of the service revolver, the cylinder was retained firmly in the frame by a cross-screw with a coin-slotted head.[7] Every feature of this revolver was over-engineered to be strong and solid, and therefore reliable, but yet the weapon was easily manipulated and not the least bit cumbersome for the soldier of that period. This set of criteria was just what the WD had wanted since the 1850s.

The Mk II

By 1894 it was realized that the original design of the Mk I revolver could be made more serviceable, more repairable and somewhat more robust. There were only very minor changes from the previous mark. The standing breech/recoil shield that had been an integral part of the Mk I's frame was

[7] One of the early manifestations of a cylinder retainer was the turnover knob type used on 'Pryse'-type revolvers of the 1870s. A 180-degree anti-clockwise turn would release the cylinder, and this position was indicated only by a small lightly engraved arrow on the release knob. In the wrong position, the cylinder was ejected along with the cartridges. Such may have been the scenario with Lt Teignmouth Melvill's 'Pryse' when he was attempting to save the Queen's Colours from the Zulus at the battle of Isandhlwana in January 1879. His revolver was found near his mutilated body, *sans* cylinder.

The Webley Mk I (top) and Mk II are shown here for comparison. Note the obvious differences in hammer and grip-frame configurations. (Author)

replaced by one that was dove-tailed into position and could be easily interchanged when worn. The lump at the top of the grip frame behind the hammer, called the prawl, was omitted. A sturdier trigger guard replaced the earlier version that narrowed on both ends of its base, and a wider spur on the hammer was adopted for easier cocking by gauntleted cavalry troopers. Internally, more reliable coil springs displaced the prior 'V' springs of the hammer catch and extractor cam assemblies. With the adoption of the Mk II (LoC §7816) all Mk I pistols were to be upgraded to the Mk II standard as the Mk I* by removing the prawl (though seldom done) and replacing the standing breeches and trigger guards in accordance with the new dictum. Concurrently with the introduction of the Mk II came the official retirement of all Adams revolvers from frontline service (LoC §7687); for the British service revolver, an epoch had ended and a new era was dawning.

THE Mk III

With a vast commercial market to supply, in addition to seeing to the military's needs, P. Webley & Son strove to refine their products and improve their business structure. To this end, Webley formed an amalgamation with the shotgun manufacturer W. & C. Scott in October 1897; this venture coincided with the introduction of the Mk III service revolver (LoC §9039). The new mark incorporated a water-hardened pawl, ratchet and recoil shield (giving these parts a greater resistance to wear), and a new means of cylinder retention/dismounting – a novel design that would be a part of every subsequent British service revolver specification until the abandonment of the revolvers in 1957 in favour of the Browning 9mm self-loading pistol.

The Mk III cylinder catch configuration utilized completely new barrel and hinge (joint)-pin assemblies. On the barrel lug, beneath the holster guides, pivoted a 'U'-shaped cylinder retainer (cam). This retainer was actuated via an eccentric tooth on the cam lever attached to the left side of the frame; the tooth rotated with the lever around the frame's hinge pin. When the frame was closed, the retainer was retracted from engagement with the cylinder axis, allowing freedom of rotation. However, as the pistol was broken open for reloading, the tooth toggled the retainer upwards to engage a flange at the front of the cylinder, holding the cylinder in place against the rearwards force during ejection. A common feature on commercial models as well, the cam lever on service weapons was locked in place by a coin-slotted screw. When released and the lever rotated upwards, the pressure on the retainer would be relaxed and the tooth would move forwards toggling it downwards, thus freeing the cylinder for its removal.

The Mk III was short-lived in military service, as the Mk IV appeared just two short years later following a period of minor martial enterprise, thus very few 'WD'-marked examples are encountered. Yet commercial variants of the Mk III seem to abound. Commercial models of the Mk III and other marks have their chamber lengths denoted on the left side of the barrel lug as either .450/.455 or .455/.476. On some early commercial Mk III revolvers, a safety-notch on the hammer (or half-cock) arrangement was also fitted. Commercially, configurations with both 4in and 6in barrel lengths and both flared square and round butts were produced.

'Inhumane' ammunition types: Mks III, IV and V

The .455in Mk III cartridge of 1898 was designed to be, and became known with some notoriety as, a 'manstopper'. Its case length was that of the Mk II round, but on the business end of its 218-grain hollow-based, square-profiled lead projectile was a caldera-shaped concavity that was designed to cause the bullet to expand upon impact. It had a rather short service life, succumbing to the paradoxical controversy during the Second Anglo-Boer War at the Hague Convention in 1899 over 'inhumane' (expanding) bullets (War Office 1907a: 228). Declared obsolete in 1902, production of the Mk III had ceased in 1900, with the WD withdrawing them from the frontline and reverting to the Mk II round for standard issue. Remaining stocks of the Mk III were subsequently expended in target practice.

The Mk IV and Mk V cartridges originated in a commercial design by Eley Bros. Although they were officially adopted only in 1912, Royal Navy personnel had been privately purchasing large quantities of this type of ammunition since 1905 for use in competitive matches at Bisley Camp, Surrey, labouring under the belief that its 'wadcutter' bullet performed better than the pointed Mk II service round (Labbett 1993: 170). The projectiles for both the Mk IV and the Mk V were 220-grain solid-nosed bullets, seated in Mk II-length cases, differing only in their alloy composition. The alloy mix for the Mk IV was the common lead:tin at 12:1; the ratio was the same for the Mk V, but antimony replaced the tin. Though designed originally and used primarily for target practice, their looks were deceiving. At the beginning of World War I many officers took stocks of Mk IV and Mk V ammunition to France with them. In short order, the Germans were regarding their use as a contravention of international conventions on the conduct of war, as noted in 1933 (SAC 1291). To safeguard national morality and perhaps the lives of the men who carried these rounds, as there were always rumours circulating of captured soldiers found with 'Dum-Dum'[8] bullets being summarily executed, the Mk IV and Mk V were withdrawn from active service, with the Mk II again filling the void.

[8] Named after Dum Dum, an Indian arsenal near Calcutta that in the late 1890s first produced the controversial blunt-nosed hollow-pointed .303in Mk III and Mk IV cartridges.

The Mk IV

Due to both its adoption (LoC §9787) in 1899, roughly coinciding with the beginning of the Second Anglo-Boer War, and to the copious numbers of this model supplied to the British forces during that conflict, the Mk IV is known with some familiarity as 'the Boer War Model'. At first glance the Mk IV appears little changed from its predecessor, but its design contained three salient differences in addition to a few minor ones. Possibly the most significant of these changes was invisible. Though vaguely described in the LoC, the barrel, frame (body), cylinder and cylinder axis of the Mk IV were made of a steel of a 'different quality', supposedly to withstand better the pressures of the new smokeless powder loading it was to chamber. Two other important, but barely noticeable, features were: a lightened hammer spur, resembling that of the Mk I, and the doubling in width (from 0.062in to 0.125in) of the rectangular slots in the cylinder's periphery for the trigger stop/locking bolts, for better engagement characteristics. The final external modification was that the angles of the frame were rounded. Internally, the height of the trigger stop was increased, and the ratchet teeth and lifting point of the pawl were hardened to resist wear. Though different, these Mk IV components could be retro-fitted on Mk III revolvers. With the adoption of the Mk IV, Webley's revolver was to continue in service unchanged for 14 more years.

The Mk V

The nitroglycerine/guncotton-based propellant cordite had been in use in British service arms for nearly two decades when, in late 1913 (LoC §16783), the Webley Mk V was adopted. This firearm's subtle differences from the Mk IV revolver were the consequences of lessons learned from the extensive use of smokeless powder and the emphasis Webley had always put on refinements to an existing pattern of weapon. The initial variant of the Mk V was virtually identical to the 4in-barrelled Mk IV, except the cylinder diameter had been increased by a mere 0.026in to tolerate better the pressures of the new propellant then in common use. Additionally, the rear circumference of the cylinder was rounded. Concurrent with the

Other than the longer barrel of the Mk V, it appears identical to the Mk IV; however, its cylinder's diameter was wider by 0.026in. (Author)

introduction of the 6in-barrelled Mk VI revolver in 1915, the final production Mk Vs were being fitted with Mk VI 6in barrels for general service issue. From 1913 on, Mk V cylinder specifications were to prevail. Thereafter, when any Mk I* or Mk II revolver was returned for repair, its cylinder, barrel, barrel catch and frame were upgraded to the Mk V standard, thus their official designations became the Mk I** and Mk II**, respectively (the Mk II* never officially existed; Chamberlain & Taylerson 1989: 27). By the time that sabres rattled on the Continent in 1914, Webley had produced more than 130,000 .455in service revolvers, excluding the multitude of commercial models that were privately purchased.

The Mk VI

At the time of its introduction in 1915 (LoC §17319), the general configuration of the Mk VI had actually existed since 1904 in Webley's commercially produced revolvers. A flared (square) butt, favoured by target shooters; interchangeable fore-sight blades of various heights on a 6in barrel; and an improved barrel catch, which would continue to keep the frame closed even after the complete failure of its cross-screw – with the exception of the reinforced barrel catch, most of these features were *de rigueur* on the earlier W.S. (Webley Service) and '05, '10 and '11 Wilkinson models. These commercial models had been offered as an alternative to the WG revolver for private purchase by officers. Although they were finished to a higher degree than their military counterparts, these were fundamentally service weapons, and in fact their serial numbers run in a block continuous with those of the .455in Mk IV. So, by 1915 the tooling-up for manufacture and the extensive field-testing of the Mk VI had already been accomplished.

From 1916 and for the remainder of World War I, the Mk VI was the mainstay service revolver. Webley's commercial production had for all intents and purposes ceased for the duration of the war by late 1915, though a few (1,500) pre-adoption Mk V and Mk VI 'Privates' had been made concurrently with the last Mk Vs. From 1915 to 1919, the firm directed its entire resources into the war effort.

Long, lean and lethal: the perfected Mk VI (1915 onwards). (Author)

THE MK VI EXPOSED

Webley Pistol, Revolver Mk VI (opposite)

1	Replaceable foresight blade	**13**	Rifling inside barrel
2	Cylinder	**14**	Chamber throat
3	Topstrap	**15**	Extractor
4	Recoil shield	**16**	Barrel catch
5	Hammer	**17**	Hammer spur
6	Barrel-catch spring	**18**	Mainspring limbs
7	Hammer catch	**19**	Stock
8	Butt swivel	**20**	Mainspring lever
9	Trigger	**21**	Hammer catch
10	Chambers	**22**	Pawl
11	Joint (hinge) pin screw	**23**	Trigger stop
12	Holster guide	**24**	Cylinder-cam lever
		25	Cylinder cam
		26	Extractor nut

The 'humane' Mk VI round

The debate over projectiles that contradicted 'the laws of humanity' (War Office 1907a: 226) didn't end for the British military in 1914, but appeared once more in 1931. At that time it involved the round-nosed 200-grain soft-lead bullet of the Mk I .380in cartridge (.38/200) for the then-new No. 2 Mk I Enfield revolver. This projectile had been specifically designed to give the smaller-calibre weapon an optimal wounding effect by tumbling in the body (not expanding) and had been exhaustively tested to that end. However, during the revolver's trial period with the Royal Tank Corps, it was noticed that if the cartridges were kept loose in an ammunition pouch, their noses had a tendency to flatten. Again, it was imagined that due to this apparent bluntness, an uncharitable enemy could mistake the distorted rounds for Dum-Dums (SAC 1291). The lead-nosed ammunition was replaced in 1938 with a lighter and more pointed

178-grain jacketed Mk II pattern, that was considered by some to be much less potent. A trend had thus been established, and subsequently the venerable .455in Mk II round was to meet the same fate as that of the .380in Mk I. The resulting Mk VI cartridge was for all intents and purposes the cordite Mk II round with a cupro-nickel-coated bullet, and was approved for service in September 1939 (LoC §B3313). A nitrocellulose-powered variant was adopted as the Mk VIz in April 1941 (LoC §B5974). These patterns of ammunition were produced by the Imperial Chemical Company Ltd, which was operating the old Kynoch factory (Labbett 1993: 173–74).

BELOW

For comparison, all the Webley service cartridges: Mk I, Mk II, Mk III, Mk IV/V, Mk VI and Mk VIZ. (Author)

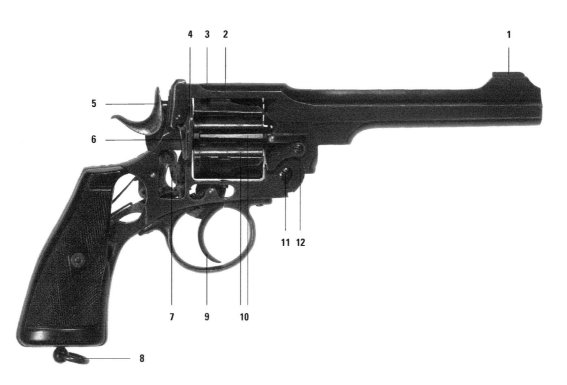

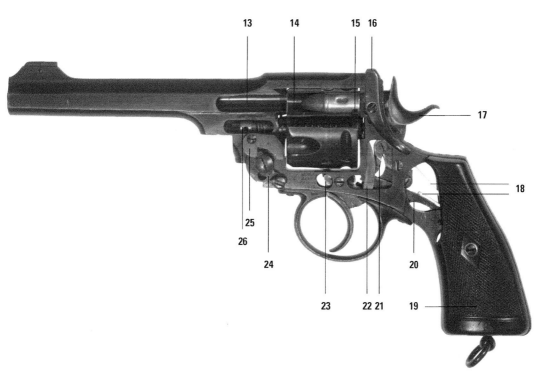

USE
A sidearm for Empire and World War

The type of warfare in which Britain was involved would change at the end of the 19th century from small, but often intense, encounters with poorly equipped indigenous armies to gruelling slugging matches with other highly industrialized nations, on battlefields where millions of soldiers would ultimately fight, and die. As the face of conflict was transformed, the hard-hitting .455in Webley was adapted to new combat techniques. These handling and shooting methods of pistols in wartime were adapted to the streets, and are even used today, when police officers will need to draw, fire and hit their target first, in a scintilla of time, to survive a close-quarters encounter with an armed felon.

THE SERVICE REVOLVER COMES OF AGE (1887–1914)

Before World War I the overall degree of discipline and shooting skill expected from the average soldier with his handgun was minimal. The allocation of revolver ammunition for training was just 24 cartridges per man per annum for all service personnel required to carry pistols (48 for cavalry), all to be expended at a single practice (War Office 1898: 131). Also allotted for practice were 5–10 rounds of blank ammunition; all told, enough to hear the revolver go bang, but not enough to gain any proficiency with a weapon. In the British Army, revolver carriage had traditionally been the exclusive domain of officers, who would provide their own weapons and ammunition, theoretically in the service calibre. However, from 1878 onwards, NCOs, cooks, trumpeters, farriers, gunners and artillery drivers were required to wear pistols. These weapons were to be carried for close-quarters self-defence, but more frequently they were used to shoot sick or disabled animals.

Service revolver practice was more or less a casual affair, undertaken with deliberate aiming at 30 paces on 8in bull's-eye targets. One-handed (right and left), well-sighted, thumb-cocked single-action fire was mostly endorsed, since double-action shooting 'when firing all the chambers rapid and continuously ... should only be adopted on emergency' (War Office 1898: 132). At least officers, having the resources to purchase their ammunition, were more inclined to practise. At the time of the Second Anglo-Boer War, due to this general lack of training among other ranks armed with handguns, it was often thought that the common soldiery wielding short-barrelled hard-hitting weapons were more dangerous to a friend than to a foe (Taylerson 1994: 18–21; Bester 2003: 71).

Curiously, during this same period there was a growing movement towards practical competitive shooting among keen pistol enthusiasts in the services and in civilian life. These competitive rifle and revolver shooting events, sponsored by the (British) National Rifle Association (NRA), were held initially at Wimbledon, then from 1890 at Bisley Camp. (This huge complex of national shooting ranges was moved from Wimbledon due to the encroachment of the city of London.) The events were the most-attended spectator sports in Great Britain at the turn of the century. Competitors could be either military, retired military, or civilian members of the NRA. All disciplines of the shooting sports were encompassed, and pistol matches began in 1885, specifically 'with the intention to cultivate military revolver shooting, for purely military purposes', according to a letter of 24 October 1888 to *Shooting* magazine (quoted in HBSA 1990: 2). These timed competitions not only involved shooting at bull's-eye targets at varying distances, but also at much more realistic advancing, traversing and disappearing targets.

One of the top competitors of the day, Mr Walter Winans, was quite a renaissance figure, being an Olympic medallist, shooting the revolver at bulls' eyes and the double rifle at running deer targets, and a celebrated (equine) sculptor. He was also a prolific writer and pontificator on just how pistols (among a myriad of other things, and all in excruciating detail) should be used. He is probably the first author on record to publish a book

Atop a *kopje* (small hill), 'Manakin' of The Royal Inniskilling Fusiliers at the south-east piquet, Belfast (Bergendal Farm, Transvaal), August 1900. This rather unorthodox militiaman appears ready for any eventuality, kitted out with a Boer bandolier and armed to the teeth with a Model 1895 7mm Mauser rifle and a Webley .455in 'WG' Army revolver. (Imperial War Museum Q 72439)

Walter Winans (c. 1904) at Bisley Camp firing his favoured S&W No. 3 Target Model. Eccentric, yes. Flamboyant, yes. But knowledgeable to the extreme. He knew how to shoot a revolver in both target and in practical situations. The somewhat distraught-appearing competitor to his left grasps, flaccidly, a Webley 'WG' Target Model. (Richard Milner collection)

The Webley 'WS' target revolver made its appearance in 1904 and, along with Wilkinson Models '05, '10 and '11, paved the way for the introduction of the Mk VI in 1915. (Author)

on the art of practical pistol shooting (Winans 1904). Winans, like most of the shooting community of that day, viewed shooting a handgun as a challenge. This challenge was to be able to shoot, initially with consistency, then with precision, at a bull's-eye target up to 50yds away. But, he also embraced many practical aspects of shooting, owning and carrying a handgun for self-defence; though at that time, he made no value judgement on when it could be used for that purpose. His basics of good handgunning were distilled down into how the pistol was gripped and how the whole hand was used to pull the trigger to release the hammer. These fundamental criteria would also be emphasized by later advocates of the tactical use of pistols, especially during World War I.

At Bisley shooting matches, both current service and civilian 'WG' Webley models were always in the medals. The reason wasn't simply that they were English revolvers and the competitions were in England, but that they were excellent weapons, pitted against the latest Colt and S&W target models of the day. Bisley provided a fertile proving ground for Webley, a company that always had an eye to improve its products. From 1904 to 1911, Webley brought out four new models of traditional revolvers aimed at the military via private purchase by officers. These were, in order of appearance, the Webley Service ('W.S.'), 'suited for the

Precursors of the Mk VI: Wilkinson Models 1905 (above) and 1911. (Author)

cavalry with its square butt', and the Wilkinson Models of 1905, 1910 and 1911. All were finished and fitted to a higher standard than service types, but these weapons were a foreshadowing of the 6in-barrelled Mk VI revolver introduced in 1915. It appears that Webley was fortunate to introduce these models in peacetime, well ahead of the future world war, thus their factory machinery was fortuitously poised to address the complaints from the trenches about the slippery round-butted earlier models.

As campaigns came and went during the last decade of the 19th century, the face of warfare was changing dramatically. Fewer enemies were armed exclusively with edged weapons and low-velocity black-powder muskets. Some of the last encounters of this type were in 1898 during the 'River War', Kitchener's reconquest of the Sudan from the Muslim followers of the Mahdi. The Dervish opponents were great in number and in religious ardour, but lacked substantial quantities of modern weapons. On 1 September 1898, the day before the battle of Omdurman, several small enemy fortified villages were occupied through the cooperation between gunboats on the Nile and troops ashore. Future British prime minister Winston Churchill recounts an incident involving a revolver during the fighting around one of these villages:

> While the attack was in progress, a party of five Baggara horsemen issued from the village and charged gallantly. Major Wortley and Lieutenant Wood were watching the fight, protected by an escort of fifty Arabs. On the approach of the Baggaras the escort fled. The two British officers defended themselves desperately with their revolvers. A horseman galloped at Lieutenant Wood, who awaited his charge pistol in hand. The Dervish leveled his broad spear, and scarcely missed the subaltern's throat by all inch [*sic*]. His outstretched arm shot over the officer's left shoulder, and the latter, meeting him in violent collision, thrust his revolver in the wild face and pulled the trigger. (Churchill 1899: 141)

Churchill was a subaltern at this time, serving with the 4th Hussars, but attached to the 21st Lancers. On the day of the major battle he took part in the immortal charge of the 21st through a dry water course (*khor*) that seethed with the enemy. Acquitting himself well, he arrived unscathed on the opposite bank, shooting at least five Dervishes, and destroying 'those that molested me'. Less fortunate were the balance of the 400-plus Lancers, who suffered 16 per cent casualties in that encounter. Otherwise the battle of Omdurman was a complete rout, ultimately decided in favour of the British by overwhelming fire from .303in Lee-Metford rifles, Maxim machine guns and artillery.

Just over a year later, the British Army was once again engaged in a far-off conflict. This time it was against the Boers, farmers of Dutch origin, in South Africa, who were armed with weapons that were the equal to – if not slightly better than– those the War Department could field. In this, the Second Anglo-Boer War, the revolver did not play a major role. In the most general terms, it was a conflict of companies of British riflemen pitted against *Kommandos* (guerrilla bands) of Boer sharpshooters. British officers, made conspicuous by their swords, were often targeted by these marksmen; the snipers were harbingers of the preferential predation meted out by the Germans some years later on the Western Front. The ability of the enemy to perform such fine shooting was in part because their Mauser Model 1895 7mm rifles shot flatter and could be loaded quicker than the Lees of the British, but possibly more important was the fact that most Boers had received a rural upbringing and had become acquainted with firearms at an early age. After the regulars of the Boers were defeated by Lord Roberts early on in the conflict, it took another two years to wear down the guerrillas to a point that induced them to make peace.

Following the hard-won Boer surrender, the War Office surveyed officers whom had served in South Africa and asked them for their recommendations on how the military could have done things better. One category in this survey regarded the use and appropriateness of handguns in combat. In the 360 responses to the 603 queries, the view of pistols as a martial weapon ranged from 'practically useless' for earlier 19th-century Colts to praising the current Webley service patterns and commending the new Mauser self-loading pistol as 'the best kind' (Bester 2003: 71–75). At that time, in 1902, semi-automatic pistols, commonly referred to as self-loaders, had been available for a decade. Early forms, such as the Model 1893 Borchardt-Luger and the C1896 'Broomhandle' Mauser ('C' stood for

One of the first successful self-loading pistols was the 7.63mm C1896 'Broomhandle' Mauser. Its narrowness made it easy to carry, its ten-shot magazine gave confidence to its owner, and its butt-stock pistol case could convert the pistol instantly into a carbine. (Author)

Construktion) were popular among serving officers; in fact Lt Churchill had carried a C96 at Omdurman and in South Africa. The Mauser, especially, was flat and thus easy to carry, had a relatively large magazine capacity (ten), and could be made into a carbine by fitting a shoulder stock/holster. The only real complaint with the Mauser was the over-penetration and thus the lack of stopping power

Designed by the immortal John M. Browning, Colt's .38in ACP Model 1900 first served some British officers in the Second Anglo-Boer War. This basic design evolved, through other successful variants, into the famous .45in ACP Model 1911. (Author)

of its small 7.63mm (.30in) bullet, though a suggestion was briefly entertained that 'in a savage war' soft-pointed ammunition might be used to improve matters (Bester 2003: 73). Other new semi-automatic pistols, for example the early Browning-designed Colt .38in ACP (Automatic Colt Pistol) Model 1900, a predecessor of the later Government Model, had made their martial appearance in this war too (Taylerson 1994: 18–21). Shortly after the conflict, the Small Arms Committee (SAC), which was then the motivating body for weapons advancement in the services, showed much curiosity in this recent development in handgun technology. This interest would continue to the time of World War I, when the Navy and the Royal Horse Artillery (RHA) would eventually be armed, to a limited degree, with Webley .455in semi-automatic pistols.

Why the Army and, in general, all the services clung to the revolver as the preferred sidearm at this time is a matter for debate. Most likely, because the Webley was a known commodity, logistically – supply could be guaranteed – and there was still much doubt about the reliability and effectiveness of new designs then appearing. The .455in service revolver was ultimately reliable and had proven stopping power, but what if a self-loading pistol could serve the same purpose? New types arose, specifically the .455in Webley-Fosbery self-cocking 'automatic' revolver in 1901. This was a design that could appeal to those unsure of the attributes of a revolver, yet it retained the familiarity of the type. Whatever its deficiencies ultimately were, such as failing to operate in the mud of the trenches, it was a novel and enticing weapon; because of its low recoil it could be shot with surgical precision, and was thus banned from many target competitions. The .455in Fosbery variant was also provided with an ammunition clip that retained all six rounds for rapid reloading, an advanced feature that would become a necessity a decade and a half later.

These new semi-automatic pistol and revolver types, such as the much-liked Colt New Service, were introduced at the turn of the century and were all available for private purchase. At that time, there was a cornucopia of pistols in use by officers. Some older gentlemen favoured double- or

multi-barrelled hard-hitting handguns or other mid-19th-century weapons like the Webley RIC, Pryse-types or the No. 5 Army Express. Others, mostly younger officers, embraced Webley WGs, or other models, commercial variants of the service revolver and newer WS and Wilkinson offerings. Before the 1915 War Office dictum of a general issue of revolvers, the Army's officers wielded a veritable plethora of pistol types.

Things were changing, however. The revolver drills described in the 1907 Naval and 1909–14 Army *Musketry Regulations* did finally call for more frequent practice, and thus the expenditure of much more ammunition, though still emphasising well-sighted deliberate single-action shots. The necessity to shoot more was a direct result from the Second Anglo-Boer War; more rounds, in general, were to be sent down range by all soldiers, and the use of (all) small arms was never again to be neglected. This was most fortunate, as in 1914–15, Britain's small but well-trained peacetime army would need to make every shot count against the juggernaut of the Imperial German Army. A general increase in proficiency with revolvers was clearly evident early in the war by this excellent demonstration of long-range shooting: 'During the retreat from Mons [August–September 1914], some isolated officers drove off a party of Uhlans [German Lancers], by opening fire on them with their revolvers at an approximate range of 250 yards, causing several casualties' (Tracy 1918: 74).

Battle of Omdurman, 2 September 1898 (previous pages)

On the morning of 2 September 1898, the battle that was the culmination of the reconquest of the Sudan by British, Egyptian and Sudanese forces erupted with fusillades from Lee-Metfords, Maxims and artillery pieces that decimated the tens of thousands of Mahdist footsoldiers on the plain before the city of Omdurman. The initial rout was brief and the Sirdar (British general Herbert H. Kitchener) wanted to get his troops into Omdurman, only 5 miles away, before the retreating Dervishes could enter in force and fortify the town. Thus, he dispatched the 21st Lancers, over 400 strong, to reconnoitre the path on his left flank into Omdurman.

They pressed forward immediately, running into only scattered groups of the retreating enemy and isolated bouts with sharpshooters. However, lying unseen in their path was a *khor* (dry watercourse) – *Abu Sant*, 6ft deep, that harboured more than 3,000 Dervishes led by Osman Digna (the name corrupted by the British from Uthman ibn Bakr Dignai). Not noticing this dead ground, the Lancers pressed forward. Suddenly, before them was a ditch full of armed men standing 12-deep in places. There was nothing to do but press on at the gallop, using the full momentum of this immense equine steamroller to carry the troopers through.

In the van was young Winston Churchill (4th Hussars, attached to the 21st Lancers) who made it through the fray unscathed. It only took two minutes to smash through the sea of angry metal, but by the time the other bank was reached, 21 men were dead, and 50 more were wounded; some, along with their exhausted mounts, were lacerated horribly. Another charge was dismissed as folly, so the squadrons crossed the *khor* below Digna's men, dismounted and opened fire with massed Lee-Metford carbines, Webley .455in revolvers and Winston Churchill with his 'Broomhandle' Mauser. The Dervishes attacked feverishly down the length of the drainage, but were thrown back by the immense weight of firepower from the Lancers. The opposition that survived melted away to the west, in the direction of Omdurman.

Holsters before World War I

Holsters were of course produced to contain the myriad of handgun types. At the turn of the century, Army officers carried their pistols in flapped leather 'cases' that afforded the weapons much protection against the elements, but little convenience for the user should he need to deploy the weapon rapidly under duress. The Navy also carried their revolvers in virtually the same manner; however, the major seams of naval holsters were riveted rather than sewn with cotton thread, which was prone to rotting when exposed to salt-laden water and moist air. Ammunition was carried loose, again, in a gusseted flapped pouch that offered the same attributes as the holster. (Though the service Webley was able to eject all of its spent cases at a flick of the wrist, rapid loading of rounds was taught and undertaken by twos – better than a gate-loaded Adams revolver, but possibly too slow when one's life was in imminent peril.) Pistol case and ammunition pouch were all part of an ingenious leather equipment ensemble (belt and braces) invented by the one-armed North-West Frontier fighter Gen Samuel J. Browne VC (1824–1901). Whatever the drawbacks, as were to appear in World War I, in the late Victorian Army the system provided a secure means of carrying an officer's pistol, ammunition and sword. Other ranks actually had things a little better, or at least more convenient, and were able to carry their revolvers in open-topped holsters that allowed more immediate access. These Land Service holsters were initially for 4in-barrelled pistols, but later this 19th-century pattern was either modified by stitching on an additional 2in of leather at the muzzle end, or made new in 1915 for the 6in-barrelled Mk VI. The last variant of the Victorian open-topped holster was introduced in 1898 as the Mk III. Due to the parsimonious nature of the War Department, all holsters in service were upgraded when there was a change in the equipment specifications. In 1896, it was thought necessary to carry a cleaning rod attached to the holster, so leather was provided to artificers, sewn on, and a channel to house the tool was made. Before 1898, revolvers were carried on the left side; after this date they were worn on the right with their muzzle-ends canted severely in that same direction, so with the introduction of the Mk III pattern, all Mk II holsters had their belt loops refitted to establish the correct jaunty angle necessary. Then with the introduction of the 1908 Mills webbing, and the obsolescence of leather belts, loops were removed for good, and provision was made for a pair of brass clasps to embrace the new 3in woven belts. Ammunition pouches also went through a similar series of modifications. They were ungusseted, thus flat in profile and holding far less ammunition than the officers' equivalent. This was probably [inadvertently] a wise feature, considering the early standard of proficiency required from the soldiers; they could do far less damage that way.

ABOVE

Officers in the Sudan wearing various iterations of Sam Browne belts, pouches and pistol cases. (Imperial War Museum HU 93831)

LEFT

The load-carrying equipment, belt and braces, designed by Gen Samuel J. Browne VC. (John C. Denner collection)

WORLD WAR I

Within the rapidly expanding Army of 1915, the issue of handguns was increased in areas not foreseen in the pre-war standing Army. Not only did this trend correspond to those personnel that had traditionally carried pistols, though now more plentiful, but also to those members of specialized units, or units with specialized weapons, where the carriage of a rifle would be too cumbersome.

Mounted troops for all ranks from sergeant upwards had customarily been supplied with revolvers. The RHA batteries were issued with 70 pistols each, with the issue to other types of batteries probably less (Thomas 2010: 9). In 1914 the RHA was making a transition away from their Short Magazine Lee-Enfield (SMLE) Mk III rifles, with the void being filled primarily with Mk IV revolvers and a dribble (only 439 by 1919) of .455in Mk 1 Nos 1 and 2 Webley autos with detachable shoulder stocks and adjustable sights (Bruce 1992: 252–64; Cuthbertson 1999: 66–71). Military Police (MP) officers, either mounted or on foot, all wore holstered weapons. The pilots and observers of the fledgling Royal Flying Corps (RFC) carried revolvers and semi-automatic pistols for personal defence, but also (in addition to rifles) as the offensive armament for their aircraft in the early days of air warfare before machine guns were commonly fitted. In 1915, one squadron reported 175 Webley revolvers and a dozen self-loading pistols in stores. In 1916, the pistol became the secondary arm for the newly formed Machine Gun Corps, when their rifles were withdrawn. Another rather specialized unit, the Tank Corps, most assuredly appreciated their handguns as their form of secondary armament. Revolvers were both convenient in the limited space inside a tank, and necessary for the tank's defence, considering the hazards inherent with crewing one of those awkward, vulnerable and extremely unreliable examples of 'modern' warfare:

The No. 1 and No. 2 at this Lewis machine-gun post have as their secondary weapons Mk VI revolvers, carried in open-top holsters of the Pattern 1914 leather equipment. Lys Canal, Saint-Venant, France, 15 April 1918. (Imperial War Museum Q 6528)

91736 L/Cpl. Paveley, W.C. 'H' Battn. Awarded M.M. [Military Medal]

For conspicuous gallantry and devotion to duty in the attack on Fontaine on November 23, 1917.

He drove his tank with the driver's flap open in spite of the enemy, who tried to bomb the tank at seven yards distance, and emptied his revolver six times in their midst with good effect.

He skilfully handled his tank to enable the gunners to bring fire upon targets which he pointed out. It would have been impossible for him to have seen the targets with the driver's flap closed. By his gallantry he was the means of inflicting heavy casualties on the enemy. (Anon 1983: 208)

The revolvers were put to many other purposes. The suffering of a large percentage of the 484,000 horses and mules that tragically became casualties during the conflict was ended with either a Webley Mk II revolver or a .310 Greener Horse-Killer carried by transport personnel. Tunnellers, also, found the revolver a convenient sidearm in the tight spaces of the shafts they dug below no-man's land to mine the enemy trenches.

Naval personnel, who were amongst the first to acquire Webleys in 1891, for shore and boarding parties, always had sufficient stocks of Webleys on board their vessels. Battleships carried 40, and cruisers between 20 and 40, depending on their class. Destroyers had 25 and gun- and torpedo-boats were issued with anywhere between 12 and 24. Since the Navy was the first to acquire the Webley, they were replete with Mk Is and Mk IIs. Naval ownership of these weapons can be readily identified by either an upper-case 'N' at the apex of their grip frames, or a crude War Department 'Broad Arrow' possession mark filed into their topstraps.

A Mk VI is clearly visible, held by a lance corporal of The Worcestershire Regiment. These men are holding the south bank of the Aisne River at Maizy, 27 May 1918. (Imperial War Museum Q 6658)

As a warrant officer of 2/10th (County of London) Battalion (Hackney), The London Regiment, gives a drink to a wounded man during the battle of Amiens on 8 August 1918, the attentive first lieutenant is carrying his service revolver in a typical flapped 'pistol case' of the period. (Imperial War Museum Q 6910)

A 1919 packet of seven .455in self-loading cartridges bearing the label 'NOT FOR REVOLVERS'. (Author)

As the years progressed, these older variants were progressively upgraded to the Mk I** and Mk II**, Mk V equivalents, by 1914 (Thomas 2010: 9 & 23). At the outbreak of war, the Navy only seemed to possess these older marks, and possibly some Mk IVs, skipping any procurement of either the Mk III or Mk V revolvers. During the war Webley also supplied over 7,000 Mk IN .455in self-loaders to the navies of Great Britain (7,041) and Australia (520) (Cuthbertson 1999: 62).

An unfortunate phenomenon was soon observed within the branches of the services where both .455in revolvers and autos were being used side by side. The cartridge case for the self-loading pistols is a semi-rimmed design and will therefore chamber and headspace in a revolver. However, if the round was fired from a revolver a sudden rise in pressure could burst the cylinder. The reason for this malady was never fully divined, as both the semi-automatic pistol as well as the revolver cartridges are theoretically low-pressure rounds. To help avoid inadvertent ammunition exchanges, wartime packets of seven .455in self-loading cartridges were prominently marked with 'Not For Revolvers'.

Alongside the increasing attrition of the conflict, Webley had always been striving to keep its production up, largely curtailing its commercial line of pistols and only manufacturing weapons for the government. Yet the firm was constantly losing skilled workers to the front. Machinery was on back order, and only belatedly materialized. Somehow, Webley was able to maintain production through adversity. Throughout the war, arms arrived from other countries – .455in Colt New Service and S&W Mk I and Mk II Hand Ejector revolvers from America in the tens of thousands, and inferior Spanish Orbea pistols in the thousands – but Webley produced their product in the hundreds of thousands for the war effort. Roughly 310,000 Mk VI revolvers were produced by 1919, when the government contracts were at last terminated; the last service Mk VI actioned, was number 445,999, on 1 July. Weekly production had grown in the four years of war from 500 in 1914 to 1,900 by 1918. This sum of all the Mk VIs, along with the 135,000 or so of earlier marks then in service, and privately purchased models, gave the Webley an overwhelming preponderance of numbers, roughly two-thirds of all the pistols fielded by the forces of the British Empire during the war (Thomas 2010: 26). Because of their high prevalence, revolver practice emphasized the Webley, in both the government's and in most of the privately printed literature.

THE ADVENT OF PRACTICAL PISTOL SHOOTING

At the beginning of World War I, the troops were fighting a fluid war of mobility until after the first battle of the Marne (September 1914), when things began to stagnate into a morass of attrition. After that, attacks became very localized and costly because of heavy shelling, enfilade fire by the copious numbers of MG 08 Maxims, and sniping. However, at times the combat became very personal indeed, when either clearing a house or a dugout, raiding an enemy trench, or having one's own trench raided.

Trench raids, to capture prisoners for intelligence gathering or to disrupt an attack before it happened, required nerves of steel and split-second reactions when coming face to face with the enemy. Due to the short range of such encounters, the pistol was the preferred firearm. Being exceedingly portable, it gave the firer the ability to engage targets quickly in a 360-degree arc; it was the submachine gun of its day. From these close-quarters encounters more practical methods of training quickly evolved. These techniques would give a competent student the ability to unleash a cascade of hard-hitting rounds at a foe, rapidly, at short range and with extreme accuracy.

With the coming of World War I, new advocates of the form of practical revolver practice that Walter Winans had initiated a decade earlier came to the forefront. This earlier training was modified to instruct students in the art of close-quarters fighting, establishing methods that would evolve into the type of shooting taught to elite military and law-enforcement personnel today.

By 1915, there were two major promoters of proficient handgun shooting: Capt C.D. Tracy and Capt J.B.L. Noel. Each had his own life experiences and background with handguns from which to draw (no pun intended), which gave the pair much intuition into the pistol's practical uses. Tracy was a student of the gunfighting techniques of the American West (and probably a personal friend of William 'Buffalo Bill' Cody), while Noel had seen some hard fighting with the British Expeditionary Force (BEF) in 1914 and was distraught over the mediocre level of revolver training in the services. Both had very convergent ideas on how the pistol should be employed in war. As a consequence, they both wrote prolifically on the subject, privately publishing many pamphlets and small books on their methods. In 1916, Tracy was able to introduce some of his views into the War Office's 1909 *Musketry Regulations'* 'Instructional Course For The Webley Or Other Pistol' by anonymously authoring its Addendum No. 3. At the culmination of hostilities in 1918, both captains had been

An officer of the Women's Royal Naval Service takes aim with her Mk VI during revolver practice in the grounds of the Crystal Palace in Hyde Park, London. (Imperial War Museum Q 18706)

making an impact on soldiers heading to the front by teaching courses at government establishments on the combat use of handguns. Tracy taught at the School of Musketry at Bisley Camp, Surrey, and Noel at the Small Arms School, Hythe, Kent. These and other schools like them – for the Tank Corps, the Machine Gun Corps, etc. – were established during the war to save lives by giving practical instruction on many aspects of modern warfare.

The type of handgun firing that was taught was referred to as 'instinctive', or point, shooting. As Winans professed, it emphasized the position of the feet (foot of the pistol hand forward and pointing towards the target, with the other at a 45-degree angle), the grip on the weapon, and the let-off, or trigger pull. What made this technique instinctive, was that firing a revolver in this manner, without the conspicuous use of the sights, was analogous to pointing or throwing a ball at a target. Pointing and throwing are largely subconscious acts that coordinate sensory inputs with motor functions to achieve a behaviour that exhibits directional accuracy towards a mark. In pistol shooting, the accuracy is derived from the precision with which the weapon is initially grasped, raised to the target, and the trigger pulled. As the student attained a level of skill with these functions, slow, deliberate aiming at bull's-eye targets transitioned into rapid single- and double-action shooting at targets approximating the dimensions of the human chest. A shot need only be accurate enough to stop an assailant, and the prize won in this competition is one's life. Thousands of officers and other ranks were trained during World War I in instinctive shooting. Few failed to reach Tracy's minimal 'War Shot' standard: 'the ability to put a shot into a 16in × 12in rectangle, in one second, at 10 yards of range' (Tracy 1918: 15).

The safe 'ready' position that the revolver would be carried in once drawn; it would be raised from this position to acquire the target and fire at it. (War Office, *Small Arms Training*, Vol. II, 1924)

Tracy and Noel demanded from their students speed with safety and accuracy, emanating from a total familiarity with their weapons. Pistols were then thought of as one-handed weapons for close encounters, and, unlike today, only held with two hands for longer distances (50yds or more), when typically shot from a prone position or with a rest. When a revolver was fired in combat, it was taught to use a straight stiff arm to absorb the recoil, to thumb-cock the pistol as it began its upward motion after the draw, then progressively squeeze the whole hand, 'like squeezing water from a sponge' (Noel 1918: 16) to pull the trigger. Discharge should occur at the top of the vertical rise, at the instant the sights came into alignment on the chosen mark, without dwelling on the sight picture. With enough practice, even firing single-action in this fashion, an average shot was able to get six hits on a man-sized target at 15yds in 12 seconds, and a crack shot was able to do the same in three seconds. Due to the inherent inaccuracy of double-action shooting, it was encouraged only at very close ranges – 5yds or less – and then from the hip. However, Noel revered those who had mastered that technique and believed that 'A quick hip shot is the most deadly adversary in the world' (Noel 1918: 28). Training was all about precision in stance, grip, draw and the rise of the pistol, combined with squeezing the entire hand to pull the trigger without jerking it. Daily instruction included muscle exercises and snapping (dry-firing) drills so soldiers were thus inculcated with every aspect of the draw and let-off. Firing became second nature, allowing the shooter to maintain concentration on the target, and not on his weapon. These drills were also to gain speed with the coordinated motion and manipulation of the revolver, familiarity with one's revolver allows the necessary speed to shoot first, and because in this instance the first who shoots has the advantage. Hitting your adversary was obviously preferred, but even the momentary disorientation left by a miss would buy enough time for a hopefully more accurate follow-up shot.

From the beginning, Tracy and Noel favoured making training as realistic an enterprise as possible. At their revolver schools, elaborate trench systems were dug and canvas houses were constructed to incorporate targets that appeared or vanished, advanced or retreated, or crossed in front of the shooter. During revolver training courses, tactics for the offence as well as for the defence were taught. The instruction included ambidextrous methods for shooting around traverses when taking a trench or around thresholds in an enemy dugout, or for clearing a house room-by-room. Instruction was given in the proper use of bullet-proof cover, like that found when firing from within shell hole, or around a wall or a tree. The art of concealment – being ensconced behind foliage or some other structure that would hide the shooter, but not stop a bullet – was explained in detail. Two-handed, long-distance (50yds or more) pistol practice was given, with the purpose of keeping the heads of a machine-gun crew down, or to stop a bomber before he could get close enough to throw his grenade.

In the revolver training courses given during the war, the lessons were taught well by instructors who knew the game, and they gave the British soldier a definite advantage in close-quarters fighting. By the end of World War I, the use of the revolver or semi-automatic pistol had risen from the considered technique of the pre-war target shooter into a discipline that

BELOW LEFT
An illustration from Capt Tracy's 1918 book demonstrating the stance and posture for 'hip shooting;' the split-second double-action firing method for exceedingly close encounters. (Author)

BELOW
With the shooter's gaze locked onto the target, this plate, from Capt Tracy's 1918 text, shows the subject (possibly Tracy himself) pointing his revolver instinctively, without the use of sights, for a demonstration of 'snap shooting'. (Author)

43

favoured the survival of those who were quick and accurate enough to shoot first, and hit their mark. As Lt Richard Hawkins of 11th Battalion, The Royal Fusiliers, recalled: 'I think that I was awarded my MC [Military Cross] for killing a German soldier. Just one. I'd been walking along a trench at Thiepval when, at a corner, I walked straight into a German officer. He whipped out his Luger, but I was slightly quicker on the draw and I shot him. It was as simple as that. One of us was going to die and I didn't want it to be me' (Quinn 1993: 24).

TOOLS FOR THE TRENCHES

In Tracy's 1916 pamphlet *Revolver Shooting In War – A Practical Handbook*, he relates his combat pistol training methods, then goes on to describe in detail various means of revolver carriage and many of the accessories that could be useful in a close-quarters fight. On the pamphlet's frontispiece Winans concurred – he commended the methods 'as being thoroughly practical, and so far as they go, in accord with his own views' – and Noel adopted much of what was suggested by Tracy in his own privately published book (Noel 1918).

Tracy formed much of his philosophy about handgun usage years earlier, when working in the western United States. From that impressionable period in his life came perhaps his most significant contribution to the assortment of practical shooting accoutrements, the adaptation of the low-slung 'cow-boy' (*sic*) 'Mexican' or 'Bucket' style of quick-draw holster to the service revolver. The traditional regulation flapped pistol case afforded ample protection for the weapon, but was slow to draw from. As Lt Robert Graves, who served with 2nd Battalion, The Royal Welsh Fusiliers, recalled:

Capt Tracy's 'Cow-Boy' or 'Mexican-Bucket' holster used specifically for the quick draw in World War I combat. (Author)

Roberts, very weak [from a groin wound], tugged at his Webley. He had great difficulty getting it out of his holster. The German fired again and missed. Roberts rested the Webley against the lip of the shell hole and tried to pull the trigger, but lacked the strength. The German had come quite close now, to make certain of him. Roberts just managed to pull the trigger with the fingers of both hands when the German was only five paces off. The shot took the top of his head off. (Graves 1998: 224–25)

The regulation holster could, however, be modified to make it more 'user friendly'. To accomplish this, much of the holster's side under the flap needed to be cut away to expose more of the revolver's butt and trigger, so they could be more easily grasped during the draw. The belt loop also needed to be raised, thus lowering the holster on the hip. Ideally, the pistol should be carried, on the strong side, 3–4in below the hip bone; there the pistol is the most convenient for the hand to grasp quickly, 'like putting your hand in your breeches pocket' (Tracy 1916: 41). Tracy didn't stop with the holster, but also recommended that ammunition should be carried in loops on the pistol belt, another view straight out of the wild American west. All of these suggestions were fundamentally sound, and there is evidence that by 1915, they were already in common practice.

Tracy goes on to mention some more subtle, and possibly controversial, details that concern the pistol's carriage. Lanyards were part of the uniform of the day, an accepted tradition in the services, and possibly a necessity for mounted troops who could accidentally drop their revolver, and would have little means of retrieving it without the use of a lanyard. Regulations indicated that the revolver lanyard should be worn around the neck, but Tracy – probably rightly – considered the lanyard to be an encumbrance,

and even a liability, in the fighting on the Western Front (Tracy 1918: 117–18). If used, it should only be employed at night or if mounted, and never attached around the neck, but around the arm, beneath the epaulettes, or centrally on the Sam Browne belt, allowing enough movement so the pistol could be used with either hand. The lanyard always had the potential to foul on the weapon or on gear; an acquaintance of Tracy lost his life when his lanyard caught the hammer of his revolver, causing a misfire at a critical moment (Tracy 1918: 118). Additionally, if worn around the neck, an opponent could use it to strangle its wearer.

Carrying the weapon for instant use was only half the battle, though. In a tight spot a soldier may need to reload quickly; if so, what was the best method, and then what options did one have if all of the ammunition had been expended or the weapon jammed? The rules were as follows. Keep track of the number of rounds fired, and top up the revolver as frequently as possible. Never advance with fewer than two or three chambers loaded. When loading single rounds into a Webley, the chamber at the ten o'clock position should be loaded first, with all of the others to follow in an anti-

Boer War veterans Maj Stephen Midgley (left), officer commanding (OC) A Squadron, and Maj Lachlan Chisholm Wilson, acting commanding officer (CO) of the Australian 5th Light Horse, in a trench on the Gallipoli Peninsula, August 1915. Both are wearing unofficial civilian pistol belts and holsters reminiscent of those worn by gunslingers of the 19th-century American West; these patterns proved infinitely practical for close-quarters action. (Australian War Memorial C00428)

Thigh-riding for quicker deployment, and khaki-covered for better concealment, a World War I flapped pistol case. (Author)

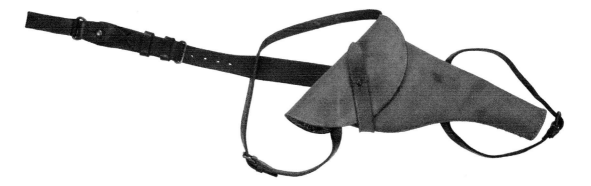

clockwise sequence. Since the cylinder rotates in a clockwise direction, when the weapon is closed and cocked the ten o'clock chamber will be rotated into the 12 o'clock firing position straight away. (This goes for the Colt New Service as well, but the S&W rotates anti-clockwise, so the crucial round needed to be loaded at the one o'clock position.) Unloading was also dealt with in this list of techniques designed to allow the revolver and its owner to work efficiently together. To unload a Webley effectively, without running the risk of a jam being caused by trapping a spent case under the extraction star, the pistol should be turned on its side or inverted when broken open.

Another option for topping up was with what is referred to today as a speed-loader, which is basically a charging device that holds the cartridges in the correct orientation for their simultaneous insertion into all of the cylinder's chambers. By 1914 there were three types available to the serviceman: the Watson, the Prideaux and the Webley Quick Loader. The Watson and the initial version of the Prideaux were patented in 1893, their development being encouraged by the introduction of the break-open Webley service revolver a few years earlier. The robust, and relatively expensive, Watson was in fact made by P. Webley & Son. William de Courcy Prideaux patented an improved version of his loader in 1914. His design, produced by the Austin Motor Company, utilized thin sheet-metal stampings and was far easier, and cheaper, than the Watson to fabricate. Typically, both types were worn on the sword belt in single or multiple pouches. During the war, Prideauxs were also sold pre-loaded in waterproofed paper pouches that could be kept at the ready in a tunic pocket or with one's kit. Webley's Quick Loader, designed by the firm's chief engineer William Whiting, was patented in 1901 and can be described in current jargon as a 'full moon clip', basically a flat brass disc with holes in it for the cartridges. Of the three, it was undoubtedly the simplest and the least expensive (sold pre-loaded in boxes of four or by the dozen), and perhaps the best, but alas, in its original configuration it could only be used with the Fosbery. To load a cylinder, the Watson needed to be inserted and its upper portion given a smart clockwise

Trench raiding, World War I (previous pages)

The British invented trench raiding, but it was refined by the Canadians, and subsequently 'stunts' became common practice among all Allied (and German) troops. Trench raiding was used with great effect to disrupt the enemy the other side of no-man's land and to capture prisoners for intelligence gathering. The raiding party struck at night, and it took nerves of steel for the attackers to make their way across an expanse of muddy, cratered and barbed-wire-laced terrain to the enemy's trench. Stealth and knowledge of the opponents' habits were vital. Noise was inevitably made – cutting barbed wire, tripping over a corpse, etc. – but *if* the noise coincided with some sort of background event, such as a distant or covering barrage, then the enemy might not be alerted. Wearing soft caps and faces blackened with soot from cooking fires, the raiders are slipping into the enemy trench, many carrying weapons that hark back to medieval times: clubs, maces and daggers. While the leading officer is holding a captured sentry at bay with the point of a Pritchard–Greener bayonet affixed to his .455in Webley Mk VI, the bomber has leap-frogged around him, to the corner of the traverse, ready to protect the party should an alert be sounded.

turn, the Prideaux simply pushed, but the Quick Loader only needed to be dropped into place.

The argument for why one design might have predominated over another is academic; the reality is that Prideaux's loader was eventually accepted into service by the War Department in 1918. The Watson and the Prideaux loaders were well designed, both were able to load any six-shot .455in revolver (Colts, Smith & Wessons, WGs and even the Fosbery) quickly in difficult conditions or in the dark, and both allowed these revolvers to compete effectively with the early automatics in speed of loading. The one huge advantage all self-loading pistols have over revolvers is that the box magazine can be

A military-marked Prideaux loader and its pouch for the Sam Browne belt. (Author)

dropped from the weapon and another inserted in seconds. Remember though, that those single-stacked magazines of World War I-era autos typically held only 6–8 rounds, a far cry from the current double-stacked varieties presently found in SIGs, Glocks, etc. So, rapid loaders gave the revolvers of that era a competitive position in an environment where self-loaders were still relatively new and generally considered not totally reliable. Depending on the type of rapid-loader, it gave the revolver shooter the ability of firing 48–72 rounds per minute.

In the heat of battle, if a revolver was empty or became unserviceable, there were still alternatives for its use. These options, as given in Revolver School lectures, all suggested immediate aggressive actions. If the revolver was known by only the shooter to be empty, then it should be used for bluffing the intended victim. Barrels of disabled weapons at intimately close quarters could be used to jab at the eyes or throat, and the sharp foresight blade on the Mk VI could be used to slash with a backhanded sweeping motion, to attack an opponent. Finally, the grip on the butt should never be relinquished and the

The Pritchard–Greener bayonet, when mounted on a Mk VI revolver, made this combination a fearsome tool for trench raiding. (Author)

barrel held for the weapon to be used like a club. There had been accounts from the trenches of officers being shot after experiencing a misfire, when they grasped their revolver's barrel for bludgeoning purposes, only to have their foe grab the butt and pull the trigger until the revolver discharged.

Trench warfare spawned a great many interesting weapons for raiding, harking back to medieval combat when clubs, hand daggers, and maces were employed: 'Few men carried rifles, since they were allowed to bring their weapons of choice, bombs were the most popular, revolvers almost as favoured, and some men brought clubs' (Rawling 1992: 102). The Pritchard–Greener pistol bayonet for the Webley Mk VI might possibly fall into this category. In late 1916, Capt Arthur Pritchard, then a lieutenant, returned to England after having served in Flanders since mid-1915. His initial idea for the bayonet was taken to the Wilkinson's Sword company, where a prototype was made, but nothing further was undertaken. Subsequently, Pritchard was able to establish a business relationship with the gun-making firm of W.W. Greener for the commercial realization of his idea. Two variants utilizing shortened French Gras rifle bayonets and scabbards were produced. Of these, the most common variety had a brass or gunmetal hilt, whereas the rarer type had a steel one. The final product did make the Mk VI appear a fearsome tool for attack, and Tracy thought it 'a thoroughly practical idea, and is of value in hand-to-hand fighting' (Tracy 1918: 115; he mistakenly thought that the Pritchard–Greener bayonet was produced by P. Webley & Son). Even so, the pistol bayonet was not a commercial success, with probably with fewer than 200 produced and even fewer being sold (Pegler 1993: 163–73). Today, due to the demand created by arms collectors, the number of current copies flooding the marketplace by far outstrips that number of originals manufactured.

Probably the most equivocal of the remora-like attachments to the Webley Mk VI was the shoulder stock. The stock was originally introduced in 1915 with the large and heavily recoiling 10in-barrelled Webley 1.5in (No. 1 Mk I) signal pistol. Interestingly, the butt dimensions of the signal launcher are the same as those for the revolver; this similarity was ultimately to foster much debate among arms collectors on the appropriateness of the stock/revolver combination. However, the shoulder stock cannot be affixed to a Mk VI correctly without a channel first being milled into the bottom left base of the pistol's butt. To give the completed attachment rigidity, with either the flare gun or handgun, the left stock iron has a rib that engages the corresponding channel in the butt, and a hook at its top that embraces the upper portion of the grip frame. Otherwise, the stock fixture attaches in the same manner as would the revolver's grips, using an identical cross-screw, but with the right grip panel being made of brass instead of vulcanite.

In recent years, numerous examples of Webley Mk VI revolvers have been found with their grip frames milled, theoretically, for attachment of the stock. At least one of these pistols is a known forgery, made up by a museum specifically for display purposes with a shoulder stock attached; however, the reason for the grooves in the others is much less apparent. Since the revolver and the signal pistol have identical grip configurations, it is feasible that the modifications to the remaining observed pistols are merely parts left over from the manufacturing process. At some point during manufacture, could surplus signal pistol frames have been turned into revolver frames, or vice versa? It was wartime and every scrap that could be turned into an arm was utilized. Alternatively, thus fitted with a butt stock, the Mk VI became a much steadier firing platform. It is not beyond the realm of possibility that these Webley 'carbines' could have been produced on a one-off basis, locally, by armourers at the front, for those who desired such a weapon. To this end there appears to be at least one example.

THE INTER-WAR YEARS: PENNY-PINCHING AND PISTOL PRACTICE

For the military in the years immediately after the war, the practical methods of pistol training that had been taught in specialized schools formed the framework within which revolver development would proceed. It is often said that victorious nations, when confronted with a new conflict, are prepared only for fighting the previous war. Ultimately, insofar as a service handgun was concerned, for Great Britain in 1939 in many ways it might as well have been 1918.

During that early inter-war period, with the continued schooling of officers and other ranks in practical shooting (War Office 1924: II.156–92; War Office 1931b: II.229–57), and with no demands from a war, refinements of the service revolver were introduced. The repetitive dry-firing drills required to be proficient in instinctive shooting took their toll in the form of broken hammer noses and bodies. In March 1920 the commandant of the Small Arms School complained of these maladies and offered two fixes for the problems (SAC 248 & 265). The first was a bit of a non-starter, however correct it was in its conception. It called for floating hammer noses, like those found on Colt and S&W revolvers imported during the war. Converting all the Webleys then in service would have been just too costly for the period, and the recommendation was dropped. What was finally adopted was the manufacture of special dummy rounds. These inert cartridges were of the typical military design, composed of white metal cases with three red-painted flutes. The difference between these and the standard pattern, say for the .303in Lee-Enfield, was that the primer pockets were filled with a vulcanized (rubber) fibre compound to absorb the shock of the hammer blow. The fracturing of the hammer bodies, typically at their double-action catch, was cured by the adoption in 1925 of a leather-cushioned protector that wrapped around the top of the hammer, dissipating its impact against the frame. The Navy had been issued with a similar device since 1893 for shipboard practice. Fundamentally, the only difference between the Navy's and the Army's was that the leather was riveted to the brass attachment to the hammer in the former type, and stapled with copper or brass wire to a tempered steel attachment in the latter.

During this same early inter-war period, in 1920 the Director of Armaments set forth a proposal for three sizes of grip panels, large, medium

Used to prevent breakage of hammer bodies, the steel Land (top) and brass Naval patterns of snap pads were fitted to revolver hammers during dry-firing exercises. (Author)

(normal) and small, which would make the Mk VI more ergonomic. As the grasp of the weapon was the initial and most fundamental aspect for good instinctive shooting, the fit of the butt in the hand of the shooter was of overriding importance to accuracy. With too large a grip, the fingers couldn't maintain a consistent hold and repetitive recoil from firing made the shot placement erratic, but with too small a grip, the finger tips touched the opposing palm and this gave a looseness to the hand that enabled the revolver to spread its shots laterally. These new stock types were adopted in 1921, and of those produced 65 per cent were medium (marked 'M'), 20 per cent small (marked 'S') and 15 per cent being of the wraparound large (marked 'L') wooden variety. Speaking for the extreme experience and aptitude of the man, Tracy had foreseen these various grip difficulties and enhancements to the Webley during the war, and had suggested their remedies or implementation, respectively, in his book *The Service Revolver and How to Shoot It* (Tracy 1918).

Unfortunately, by midway through the 1920s the vast reduction of the post-war armed services and severe budgetary constraints had dissipated much of the emphasis and intensity in the military for practical revolver shooting. Many of the tools of this form of training were luxuries that could be ill afforded and were made obsolete: large stock panels in 1924 and Prideaux loaders in 1926. In the immediate post-war period, service revolvers were in short supply, but there were still practical demands for their use. During the conflict, Webley had just barely met the Army's demand for revolvers, and the Navy's for self-loading pistols. The factory's service pistol production had to be supplemented with imports from the United States and Spain. In 1920, civil wars raged in Ireland and in Russia; the rebels and communists there were perceived as anarchists, and events in both of these countries appeared to threaten the British way of life. Even in India, Britain's most prized possession, Bolsheviks were thought to be lurking and threatening to incite the more militant factions of that country's movement towards self-determination. At home, things were far from peaceful; massive unemployment and strikes gripped the land. Partially as a response to this domestic turmoil, in 1921 legislation restricting firearms ownership was implemented. This act proved to be a tremendous disincentive for the general public to possess handguns and for Webley to produce them. For this once-great firearms manufacturer, during the inter-war years 70 per cent of its efforts were re-allocated to general engineering and the automobile industry (Milner 2008: 32).

Webley would soon be dealt worse blows, this time from a sector that the company had depended on for decades. In response to the military's need for revolvers, the government set aside funds for 20,000 pistols, 16,000 of all types purchased from demobilized servicemen answering a public advertisement, and 4,000 newly manufactured (Chamberlain & Taylerson 1989: 32–33). Yet in a set of rather disingenuous moves, Parliament in 1919 accused Webley & Scott of making excessive wartime profits, then directed the Royal Small Arms Factory (RSAF) at Enfield, Middlesex, to produce the required service revolvers. Nearly 27,600 of the 'Enfield' Mk VIs were eventually made (Chamberlain & Taylerson 1989: 70), having initially no prefix, then an 'A' or 'B' prefix to their serial numbers that ranged from 1–9999 in each series (theoretically B7600 being the highest reached). The RSAF's revolver specifications were for all practical purposes identical to those of the Webley Mk VI, with the one real difference being that the hole for the recoil shield screw penetrated only halfway through the body. They were manufactured from 1921 to 1926, and can immediately be identified by: 'Enfield', the Royal cipher, the mark designation, and year of manufacture impressed onto the right flat of their frames below the hammer. In 1926 the LoC (§A1636) listed new nomenclatural designations for swords, pistols and lances, thus the 'Pistol, Revolver, .455in Webley Mk. VI' was reborn as the 'Pistol, Revolver, No. 1 Mk. VI'. More bad news for Webley was just around the corner.

The restrictive economic parameters within which the military had to operate during the inter-war years influenced all new small-arms development to a greater or lesser degree. Pistol practice using .455in rounds was expensive, and often it took the uninitiated soldier quite some time to become accustomed enough to the recoil of the service revolver to shoot with any accuracy. An additional concern about the .455in Webley was that it was, by 20th-century standards, exceedingly expensive and rather complicated to make. During World War I, Webley's output had been bottlenecked by 19th-century engineering techniques for the revolver's manufacture; with great prescience the SAC considered two options that would make the production of a service handgun easier in the next war, whenever that might occur (SAC 462). The first was the simplification of the existing Webley design, while the second was the introduction of a new service type in .38in. On 19 July 1921, a representative from Webley & Scott

Enfield's Design Department's drawing (D.D. (E) 29) of their Webley-equivalent .380in 'Experimental'. (© Royal Armouries)

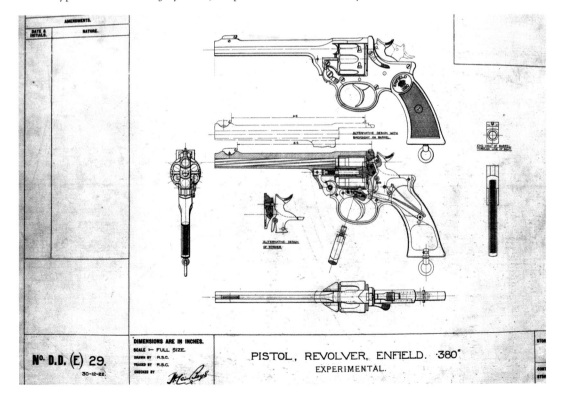

The Webley 'Experimental Model' Mk IV .380in revolver, as supplied to the War Office in 1921 – soon to be the Enfield No. 2 Mk I revolver. (Small Arms School Corps Museum, Warminster)

had delivered an 'Experimental Model' Mk IV .380in revolver to the War Office (SAC 428). Since then the SAC had been debating the pros and cons of each course of action, then eventually in December 1922: 'The [Small Arms] Committee recommend that the development of the .380-inch pistol should have precedence over any modifications to the .455-inch design' (SAC 518). When compared to their standard commercial Mk IV, several refinements, such as a sideplate, floating hammer nose and a single cylinder locking bolt/stop, were incorporated in Webley's submission. These new features were to help make the new weapon less expensive to manufacture, yet maintain its inherently robust design; just what the War Office wanted, or so Webley thought. (Indeed these embellishments somewhat modernized the weapon, but could hardly be thought to simplify its manufacture.)

Though there were some minor difficulties with the initial weights of the single-action pull-off and trigger cocking, the only really significant complaints proffered by the members of the SAC were: 1) they thought the grip needed to be enlarged for better control during instinctive shooting; and 2) they were concerned about the stopping power of the smaller projectile, as compared to the .455in bullet. Webley subsequently obliged the SAC by making modifications to its design and submitting two revolvers (that didn't reach the Small Arms School until March 1924), then persevering through numerous ballistic trials of their pistols. In 1923, however, the Superintendent of Design at RSAF Enfield (Capt H.C. Boys) had produced two sets of drawings (D.D. (E) 29 and 29A; D.D. (E) 29 is shown above) describing the Webley in terms of an 'Enfield .380" Experimental'. The weapon illustrated in those drawings was obviously destined to become the No. 2 Mk I revolver. By 1928 the ties that had bound Webley to the War Office for 40 years had broken. Webley & Scott challenged the government for its indiscretion and was subsequently given £1,200 by the Royal Commission on Awards to Inventors; this meagre amount was slightly over half of Webley's development cost for their

'Experimental' Mk IV (Chamberlain & Taylerson 1989: 42–45).

Revolver training with the .455in Mk II round had become so expensive by 1922 that the allocation of this cartridge was so small as to restrict instruction to the pre-war level of a single annual session (SAC 474). To cut down costs and to maintain the frequency of practice, the use of .22in rimfire ammunition was briefly entertained. None of the proposed strategies to accomplish this ideal were without their problems. Initially, a permanent conversion of the service revolver was put forth, but rejected as being too expensive in addition to depleting, by conversion, an already scarce commodity (SAC 474). A purpose-built Webley Mk VI .22 revolver was additionally tried and rejected for all the same reasons as the sub-calibre conversion of the service revolver had been (SAC 560). Concurrently, the use of Webley's single-shot aiming tubes (barrels inserts with chambers that replaced the cylinder) had also been suggested, and this approach showed great promise for a number of very sound reasons:

(i) Both 'single' and 'double' action can be practised.
(ii) The accuracy is sufficient for service shooting, and the firer is not likely to be discouraged by the results of his shooting.
(iii) As the firer would use his own pistol, the 'pull-off' will not be different when firing .455 ammunition.
(iv) Instruction in the first two practices of the annual course can be given in a miniature range. In other words, the man can be taught and practised in the fundamental principles of pistol shooting – the vertical lift and correct trigger release.
(v) The saving of .455 ammunition resulting would allow more practice of quick shooting against more than one target to be fired.
(vi) Flinching, due to anticipating the shock of discharge, would be eliminated, thus leading to more correct trigger pressing. (SAC 516)

Though the aiming tube showed great economy, since only a single round could be fired before reloading, it unfortunately couldn't be used in the final stages of training a practical pistol shot, when consecutive rounds needed to be fired. Subsequently Parker-Hale's six-shot cylinder/barrel tube

The type of purpose-built commercial Webley Mk VI .22in revolver, with a long cylinder, which was tested at the Small Arms School in 1922 in the attempt to find an economical training weapon. (Robert Taylor collection)

adapter was tried, with this combination possibly being the best all-round expedient that the SAC would find. It gave the firer multiple shots, and when fitted and filled weighed roughly the same as a service revolver loaded with .455in ammunition. The particular problem with this design was the slight reduction in accuracy due to the necessary canting of its chambers. This allowed the primer-containing rims of the smaller-diameter cartridges to be in the correct position to be struck by the hammer nose when the revolver was discharged. The slight angle (15 degrees) inclined the nose of the bullet downwards, thus when fired it had to turn a corner, or ricochet, as it entered the barrel. The resulting distortion of the projectile lessened accuracy (the group size at 10yds being roughly twice that of the converted revolver), yet not to a disheartening degree for service shooting.

So encouraging was this line of inquiry that the RSAF produced a similar cylinder/barrel adapter (D.D. (E) 227), though with a concentric bore and firing chamber. To align both chamber and barrel without angling the cartridges, the Enfield configuration needed a separate breech plate containing an auxiliary firing pin for the cylinder. The plate's pin pivoted and would transmit the energy from the strike of the hammer's nose (above) to the primed rim of the .22's case (below); in the shape of an upside-down 'L', when its top was hit by the hammer, its bottom kicked out and struck the .22's rim.

Once fabricated and put through its trials in 1924, Enfield's contribution showed very acceptable accuracy, but it was complicated, made up of 14 parts, and expensive to manufacture. This was not quite the ideal that the SAC had been striving for, so the Committee pursued yet another iteration that functionally brought them full circle to where they had started their quest for a .22in training option three years earlier (SAC 683). Two sample revolvers were to be constructed by the RSAF (D.D. (E) 480). They were to utilize existing service revolver frames and contain only four newly made parts: barrel, cylinder, extractor and foresight; in essence converted Mk VIs, and supposedly produced for less cost than any of the previous alternatives. When finally tried on 19 September 1927, both pistols exhibited superb accuracy, yet were stricken with the same set of afflictions – jams and misfires – that the Parker-Hale and Enfield six-shot adapters and both of the Webley .22in revolver submissions had suffered (SAC 862). These were all-too-common maladies caused largely by the extreme variability in the

Proposed tools for economical revolver practice during the inter-war years: the .22in single-shot Webley aiming tube and Parker-Hale six-shot adapter for service revolvers. (Author)

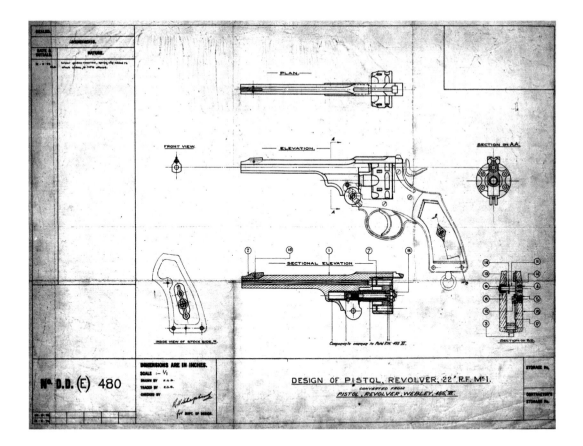

manufacturing standards of .22in rimfire ammunition of that era. By that time the .380in No. 2 Mk I revolver was a going concern, with it promising to become, shortly, the next service pistol. So, considering all of the teething troubles incumbent in the endeavour of converting the .455in to .22in, that enterprise was destined to be on the back burner for ever.

This is a design drawing (D.D. (E) 480) by Enfield of a proposed conversion of a .455in Mk VI revolver to .22in. The two revolvers produced from this drawing showed favourable accuracy, but were prone to jams and misfires, as were all the other .22in options the Small Arms Committee had entertained. (© Royal Armouries)

ANOTHER WAR, ANOTHER CALL TO DUTY

Commercially, between the wars Webley & Scott had supplied quantities of Mk VI 4in- and 6in-barrelled revolvers to the RIC, and subsequently to the police and armed forces of the Irish Free State, with the numbers of 4in police weapons appearing between just below 450,000 and about 454,000 (Bruce 1992: 207). Those 6in-barrelled Mk VIs found with their original serial numbers cancelled out and replaced with an 'N'-prefixed four-digit one are probably ex-Irish armed services (Chamberlain & Taylerson 1989: 70). Webley & Scott was able to maintain some sales of its weapons during this lean period to offshore buyers. The Royal Canadian Mounted Police (RCMP), Shanghai Municipal Police (SMP), Iran and the Kingdom of Siam, among others, were also recipients of Mk VIs. The serial numbers of these weapons are in a range between 452,000 and 454,000, and are interspersed with those of 'W.S.' 7.5in-barrelled target revolvers, referred to then as the

A man inspecting the bore of a Mk VI at the Webley & Scott factory in Birmingham during the early days of World War II (15 November 1939). (Imperial War Museum HU 36674)

'Bisley Target Revolver, Mk VI. .455' in period catalogues. Webley's October 1939 catalogue still listed the Mk VI and its .22in single-shot (aiming-tube) adapter.

During the two decades preceding World War II, the Mk VI soldiered on with British and Commonwealth forces, but the days for the previous marks were numbered. A mere trickle of spares were produced for the Royal Air Force (RAF), the Admiralty, India and South Africa, but these were nothing of consequence for Webley & Scott. As the inter-war years progressed, it was increasingly difficult to keep weapons in service, as spare parts were becoming scarce. In 1921, Webleys of all marks were considered beyond local repair if only their recoil shields needed replacement (LoC §23958), and any shields still with unit armourers were to be returned to RSAF, Enfield. A few Mk IVs that remained in naval service were converted to the Mk V/Mk VI standard as the Mk IV** in 1924 and 1925 at Enfield, but by the time of the nomenclature change in 1926 (LoC §A1636), with some Mks I–V then in service, these older patterns were considered obsolete for future manufacture, and were denoted as such in the 1931 *Instructions for Armourers* (HMSO 1931). The 1937 *Instructions for Armourers* (HMSO 1937) and a small-arms training pamphlet from that same year (reprinted in HMSO 1941) still included the Mk VI as a frontline weapon.

Unfortunately for Webley, from July 1932 on (LoC §A6862), the .380in No. 2 Mk I was 'the' service revolver, and would continue officially to be so until 1957, and functionally thereafter until 1967, when it was replaced fully by the L9A1 9mm FN/Browning Hi-Power semi-automatic pistol.[9] Within the volumes of the 1924 and 1931 *Small Arms Training* manuals, revolver practice still 'officially' embraced the 'instinctive' shooting method of World War I with all of its trappings of dry-firing drills, complex targets and realistic ranges (HMSO 1924: 156–92; HMSO 1931b: I.229–57, IV.80–86, V.105–13). Following its introduction, pistol instruction for the No. 2 Mk 1 revolver, with its rudiments based in instinctive rapid firing, largely continued as it had been taught for the No. 1 Mk VI. But by 1936, with the growing threat of a strong Germany coming (again) to the fore, Britain belatedly started to re-arm and recruit. Though civilian target pistol shooting had shown a slight increase in popularity in the 1920s, restrictive British handgun laws had kept the general popularity of this sport to a minimum in England, and few of the

[9] I am grateful to Captain Peter Laidler, Small Arms School Corps, Warminster, UK, for this information.

new soldiers had ever handled, much less fired, a pistol. As a result, both revolver training and the revolver itself were modified to suit this reality. The inherent discipline involved with rapid thumb-cocking during single-action shooting was thought too complicated, and possibly too hazardous, to teach to inexperienced personnel, and thus trials began in 1937 in which the spur and bent were removed from the .380in pistol's hammer, allowing only double-action firing (OC 85: 21). Its grip featured a modification with thumb-grooved stock panels that 'ensures a firm grip, and the pistol is less liable to move in the hand' and 'It can be quickly gripped from the case and the groove assists in obtaining the same grip each time' (OC 85: 22–24). The resulting pattern was adopted in 1939 for both land and naval use as the 'Pistol, Revolver, 0.38 inch, No. 2 Mk I*' (OB 255: 37; OB 645).[10] Subsequently, instinctive shooting techniques remained in World War II-vintage training pamphlets for the .380in revolver, but were in a much-distilled form that emphasized double-action firing (War Office 1941: 3 & 5). The 1941 version of this text did incorporate two footnoted references to subtleties that were uniquely associated with the .455in weapon, namely two sizes of stock sides and the dismounting procedure for the cam-lever fixing screw; but these were to be deleted by the time of the 1942 printing (War Office 1942). Even with a war in progress, the .455in service revolver was, apparently, on the wane.

An assembly line of Mk VI revolvers being refurbished at the Webley factory in Birmingham during late 1939. (Imperial War Museum HU 36675)

After World War I stocks of the Mk VI were depleted in Britain, but Australia, New Zealand, South Africa and Canada still held significant numbers of Webleys, along with .455in Colt New Services and S&W Mk II Hand Ejectors, in their inventories. In February 1940, the Ministry of Supply announced a requirement of 233,541 pistols for land service to fight the current war. As the No. 2 revolvers were then in short supply, orders were placed between January and June 1940 for 26,000 .455in revolvers to be repaired to war reserve standard at Enfield and by Webley & Scott. These weapons were scoured from all sources. The trade was only able to supply a few hundred. However, the Royal Navy and the RAF still held a large number of service revolvers, so much so that the Admiralty was able to release a substantial stock of weapons to Enfield for repair for the Army shortly after hostilities began (Chamberlain & Taylerson 1989: 38). As of September 1943, somewhere between 10,000 and 15,000 .455in revolvers had been repaired.

---

[10] I am grateful to Mr Ian Patrick for uncovering this information.

A World War II-vintage Webley service issue Mk IV .38in 145/200 revolver. This weapon was more akin to a scaled-down .455in Mk VI in its manufacture. It was without a sideplate and the single cylinder stops of Webley's earlier Mk IV 'Experimental Model', thus it bore little mechanical similarity to the Enfield No. 2 revolver, though both were issued in the services concurrently. (Author)

From 1940 until the end of World War II, Webley & Scott's principal efforts were for the production of 1.5in signal pistols and .380in (military and police) Mk IV revolvers for the services. To this end, the firm manufactured (with the wartime codes of M264 and M265 respectively) nearly 150,000 flare guns and 172,000 Mk IVs, along with parts for Sten submachine guns and complete fencing muskets (Milner 2008: 33). Webley also turned out barrels and spares for repair of .455in Mk III, Mk IV and Mk V pistols. During the war years other manufacturers also provided valuable components for these large revolvers; Enfield produced barrels and most major assemblies for the No. 1 Mk VI, with J. Dickenson & Sons and S. Wright & Sons producing only minor components (e.g. springs and hammer catches) (Skennerton 1988: 24–25). Other than having been assembled from existing parts or refurbished, there is no concrete evidence, as yet, indicating complete .455in weapons being produced anew by either Webley & Scott or at Enfield during this period (Chamberlain & Taylerson 1989: 38).

Throughout the 'Phoney War' and subsequently in the opening stages of the conflict, No. 1 Mk VI revolvers were common in the frontline, especially in the Middle East and China–Burma–India theatres. In the early months of 'holding the line' in Burma in 1942, a 1916-vintage Mk VI was used by Maj L.W. Bowley RAA (Royal Australian Artillery) to despatch a troublesome enemy sharpshooter:

> Bowley rejoined his regiment at Arakan in June [1942] and was promoted to major the same month. He was placed in command of a Light Anti-Aircraft battery. During this period, Bowley was shot by a Japanese sniper who was positioned in a tree. The round passed through Bowley's ribs and missed all of his vital organs. Incensed, Bowley found and killed the Japanese soldier. The Japanese soldier had been using an old single shot rifle, and was unable to reload his weapon before Bowley reached him. (Photograph caption, Australian War Memorial, ID number REL39717)

POST-WAR SERVICE

Later in the war, it appears that many .455s were still in use, but largely relegated to guards, police and secondary and support units, such as those of the RAF ground controllers and the anti-aircraft batteries of the RA, for personal defence. After World War II, the Mk VI was retained by the Royal Navy, but was made obsolete for land use in 1948. Then with their complete obsolescence in 1949, 62 years after their introduction, the era of

martial use for the .455in Webley revolvers in British service was finally over. It had been quite an amazing run, considering the technical advancement that occurred through those six decades. Granted that the Inglis/Browning Hi-Power semi-automatic pistol has now a minimum of 50-plus years of service behind it with the British and Commonwealth forces (this not including its limited use during World War II). The only pistol truly to surpass the .455in Webley for being in constant use would have to be the Colt Model 1911/1911A1 (1911–90) of the United States.

Pakistani police foiled an assassination attempt on their prime minister on 1 April 2004. Here, an officer holds weapons recovered from an apprehended Islamic militant; all the revolvers are Webleys, and at least two are .455in weapons. (Syed Zargham/ Getty Images)

The combat use of the .455in Webley didn't precipitously stop with its official obsolescence 'on paper' in the late 1940s; serving officers (mostly Royal Navy personnel and Commonwealth soldiers), continued to privately purchase and carry the revolver in the decades following the war. In the Korean conflict, and even into the Vietnam War,[11] there is evidence of its isolated use by individuals who wanted a hard-hitting weapon and who were comfortable with, and trusted, the reliability of a revolver. The final sale of a large-bore Webley revolver was on 10 April, 1964; it was a Mk VI, and its number was somewhat appropriately just over the 455-thousand mark at 455,366.[12] Webleys have also become tools for less orthodox forms of combat, both in the streets and on new and different battlefields; unfortunately, this is in evidence primarily through vivid media images of confiscated weapons caches associated with criminal or terrorist activities, most recently in troublespots like Pakistan, Afghanistan and Iraq. Everywhere Britain once had influence, the Webley was present, was trusted, and was (and still is) used as a fighting tool.

[11] Posthumous thanks to Mr Charles McEldery (USA) for his previously noted recollection of a
New Zealand officer who carried a .455in Webley & Scott revolver in the Vietnam War.
[12] I am grateful to Mr Richard Milner for uncovering this information.

IMPACT
The Webley legacy worldwide

From the introduction of the first Mk I in 1887, the .455in Webley was a continual presence in service both as a tool of war and as an instrument of change for the greater part of a century. Even though nearly every other Western national military had, in the first few decades of the 20th century, adopted self-loading pistols to arm their soldiers, Britain clung to its revolvers, for a variety of reasons. It speaks volumes for the serviceability of Webley's basic design that it made the transition from .455in to .380in in the 20th century as requirements changed; the rudiments for both the smaller Mk IV and No. 2 revolvers had evolved from those first incorporated in the .455in Webley at the end of the 19th century. The design was obviously rugged and adaptable; however, it wasn't just the inherent plasticity of the configuration that accounted for its longevity in service, but also the survival of tactics that had initially been developed for a revolver's use in battle.

For the British between the wars, both pistol practice and development stagnated; this had nothing to do with the lack of desire of the General Staff, but was largely a consequence of the lack of available funding for anything but the bare necessities of training. Aside from a brief, albeit serious, flirtation in 1937 by the SAC with the French Model 1935A 7.65mm semi-automatic (SAC 1647 & 1660), by the time trumpets sounded again in 1939 nothing truly significant had been accomplished to 'modernize' matters in terms of a service handgun. This isn't to say that the services then were entirely devoid of self-loading pistols; several thousand Colt M1911s that had been retained by the Royal Navy and RAF after World War I were carried through to World War II, with an additional 40,000 or so Colts, mostly M1911A1s, added before 1945 by the United States' Lend-Lease programme. A trickle of 9mm Inglis/Browning Hi-Powers had also been contributed by Canada in the closing months of the

war. Largely, these semi-automatic pistols gravitated towards specialist units – commandos, airborne soldiers, covert SOE operatives and the like – so in the most general terms, for the British it was still a revolver's war.

As already noted, the practical 'instinctive' defensive combat-shooting techniques that were refined between 1914 and 1918 were again carried on to the 1939–45 battlefields in a much diluted, but nonetheless effective, form for which the Enfield No. 2 had been adapted. Shooting first and pouring as many accurate follow-up rounds into your target as quickly as humanly possible proved to be sound practices for those interested in surviving an encounter with the enemy, and these dicta were ultimately to transcend eras, other wars and other weapons. A venerable Texas Ranger, Bill Jordan, sums up this philosophy quite succinctly as 'There are no second place winners.'

During World War II, the submachine gun took over many of the revolver's duties and thus, in doing so, inherited its lethal applications in close-quarters fighting. These small, fully automatic weapons filled the same niche as the revolver had filled throughout World War I. Personnel who had previously been armed with handguns – for example, motor-transport drivers and both commissioned and non-commissioned officers – began to relinquish their pistols in favour of pistol-calibre full-auto guns. The time was advanced by a score of years, but the techniques for combat had remained unchanged.

A group of Australian NCOs, possibly of the 20th Light Horse (The Victoria Mounted Rifles), lined up for revolver practice with their Mk VI revolvers aboard a transport ship early in World War II. Note the leather ammunition pouches and lanyards, vestiges of World War I. (Australian War Memorial 000586)

LAW ENFORCEMENT: IRELAND AND SHANGHAI

Ireland and Shanghai may seem as disparate in likeness as they do in geography, but they were irrevocably linked during the 1920s and 1930s in terms of their political and social upheaval and their police forces. Away from the arena of the battlefield, the .455in Webley was used with equal prowess by law-enforcement officers in countries seething with civil unrest and in cities where miscreants ruled the night.

During these decades, both Ireland and China were undergoing the bloody growing pains of countries moving towards self-determination. To maintain order in the streets or countryside where Great Britain had influence, tough paramilitary organizations existed – specifically in these instances, the RIC and the SMP. Their structures were not terribly divergent from others that existed in slightly more placid areas of the British Empire, such as those of the RCMP, Victoria Police Force (Australia), and the Hong Kong Police; but there was much more bloodshed at that time in southern Ireland and in Shanghai than anywhere else, so their techniques needed to be tough, practical and merciless to counter constant attack and incessant social turmoil.

The Irish Constabulary's origins, as the principal policing force in Ireland, dated back to 1822, with Queen Victoria contributing the 'Royal' to the constabulary in 1867. In the 20th century, the RIC had been under a more or less continuous assault from the Irish Republican Army (IRA); since 1916, barracks had been burned and officers ambushed. In China, the SMP had been in existence since 1854, 12 years after the international settlement (Treaty of Nanjing) that allowed Europeans ports and residence in five cities in this previously forbidden country. But in the post-war milieu, fighting between warlords, the Chinese Communist Party (CCP), the nationalist Kuomintang (KMT) under Chiang Kai-shek, and eventually against the militaristic Japanese, threatened the conspicuously Western community of Shanghai. As China's civil war played out through the inter-war years, during respites, the CCP and the KMT found Shanghai a ready source of finance for their respective movements, through thievery (Bickers 2004: 176–77). About Shanghai, it was written: 'armed crime flourishes here to a degree that we think must be unequalled anywhere else in the world' (Fairbairn & Sykes 1987: 2).

The RIC and SMP were intertwined in numerous ways. Both were set up with a quasi-military structure, incorporating strict discipline, uniforms and weaponry. Also, the SMP depended initially on the RIC for training of its cadets and supplying many of its officers. In the early post-war period, Webley & Scott .455in revolvers were used to arm the constables

A commercial 4in-barrelled Mk VI revolver from the inter-war years. Weapons of this type were supplied to the Royal Irish Constabulary in the early 1920s. (Author)

of both forces. The 4in-barrelled commercial Mk VI revolvers then supplied to the RIC eventually became the property of independent Ireland's *Garda Síochána* (Keepers of the Peace) after the RIC's disbandment in January 1922 (on the backstraps of these post-independence weapons are found the letters 'GS').

Shanghai's police continued to evolve after World War I, until their final dissolution at the hands of the Japanese forces in February 1943. Ever-increasing encounters with armed criminals and demonstrators motivated the SMP to develop SWAT-type techniques, riot-control measures and even 'soft' body armour, in the form of (broomhandle) Mauser-proof vests. This article of clothing would reduce the lethal effects of the 7.63mm (.30in) Mauser pistol bullet, which was known for its qualities of penetration and tissue damage.

In this era certain individuals came to the forefront and were destined to leave their marks in the field of close-quarters combat. Perhaps the most famous of these were William Ewart Fairbairn and Eric Anthony Sykes. Sykes was head of the sniping section for the SMP, and Fairbairn was in charge of weapons training. As a team, while with the SMP, they used their collective knowledge of Asian martial arts to develop armed and unarmed techniques to counter a foe at intimate ranges. Subsequently they carried these combat methods into World War II, where they trained elite soldiers and covert operatives for the British commandos and the SOE, and for the US Rangers and the OSS, from 1941 onwards. One product of their joint labours was the development of the immortal Fairbairn–Sykes fighting knife. But, back in dirty old Shanghai, they took and refined those instinctive shooting methods and training practices that Tracy and Noel had taught a few years before and adapted them for their constables who patrolled the dimly lit streets and alleyways of that port city.

Fairbairn, an ex-Royal Marine who had joined the SMP in 1907, admitted that military life 'hadn't prepared him for the roughness of life on the Shanghai beat' (Bickers 2004: 73). SMP officers were masters of instinctive shooting, essential in a city where their trade might involve felling an armed robber or clearing an opium den. The drills were basically

BELOW LEFT
The 'one-handed hold' for instinctive firing. (War Office, *Small Arms Training*, Vol. II, 1924)

BELOW
The 'two-handed hold' for long-distance shooting. (War Office, *Small Arms Training*, Vol. II, 1924)

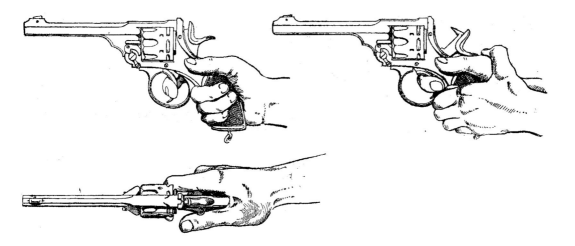

the same as in the trenches: shoot first, then shoot twice, practise on moving and disappearing targets, and perfect house clearing, which involved working around threatening corners, thresholds and corridors, places where an opponent might be lurking. One new variable that was taken into consideration in this unique world of civilian threats was the increased possibility of encountering non-shooters, bystanders and hostages; this particular variable lives on today for first-responding law-enforcement SWAT teams facing these same basic tactical scenarios.

Initially, in the 1920s SMP constables commonly carried the 6in-barrelled Mk VI revolver in a flapped holster on a Sam Browne equipment belt (these Webleys bear 'SMP' and an inventory number on their grip frames). Handguns they later adopted included the Colt .45in Government Model and New Service for constables, and Colt M1908 Pocket .380in semi-automatic pistols and snub-nosed .38in Detective Special and New Service revolvers for inspectors. Many of these cut-down, short-barrelled pistols were instantly identifiable by the lack of the front of their trigger guards, as 'Fitz Specials', specifically designed by the Colt employee J. Henry Fitzgerald for the quick-draw. For these weapons, inspectors used shoulder and inside-the-belt holsters that assisted in rapid deployment of their handguns. As in wartime the first shot mattered, and so did follow up shots: 'The more closely our own pistols resemble machine-guns [sic] the better we like it' (Fairbairn & Sykes 1987: 80).

It wasn't only speed, but also reliability that mattered. While the Webley was in common usage, the major complaint with this firearm was the use of 'V' springs, especially pertaining to the barrel catch. In practice, the 'V' spring proved to be much less robust than coil springs. The Webley's Victorian engineering was (finally) being surpassed by that of the 20th century. Fairbairn and Sykes were always keen to modify weapons to make them quicker to deploy for that first critical shot; to this end they disliked safety catches on semi-automatic pistols (Fairbairn & Sykes 1987: 14), and suggested pinning those of issued weapons in the 'off' position,

Shanghai, 1925 (opposite)
Following the bloody 30 May 1925 attack by rebellious communist-leaning students on the Louza (Nanking Road) Shanghai Municipal Police (SMP) station, unrest bubbled up into the streets of the European community. Anti-imperialist repercussions from this single incident created a surge in labour strikes and violent crime that was to last through to the end of the decade. Armed robbery and murder rates rose as money was needed to buy arms for a war for nationalism. Trouble lurked in the dark alleyways and avenues of that rough-and-ready port city.

In an incident typical of that period, a communist sympathiser has forced his way into a clock shop from a back alley, and is now emerging from the entrance, holding a bag of cash that he has just stolen from the till. Unfortunately for him, an SMP constable was on his rounds nearby, when the officer heard the commotion (a shop keeper's shout of: 'Chi'ang-Tao' – 'Robber!'). With pistol drawn, the policeman confronts the miscreant and fires his Webley Mk VI instinctively from the 'Three quarter – Hip' position, learned from his musketry instructor W.E. Fairbairn. In the background, the proprietor of the store is startled by the sudden drama playing out in front of him. The thief recoils from the impact of a heavy .455in round, and with back bent, drops the valise and the Mauser pistol he was carrying onto the pavement.

A modification to increase reliability, a coil spring-powered barrel catch on Shanghai Municipal Police Mk VI – 'SMP 637'. (Joe Salter Jr)

and letting thorough training compensate for their absence. For the Mk VI in SMP issue, barrel catches were fitted with coil springs.

In the final reckoning, Fairbairn and Sykes' training methods showed dividends in terms of constables' lives saved and criminals felled. During a 12-and-a-half-year period, with no fewer than 666 encounters with armed criminals, the advantage given to SMP officers from their weapons training was evident (Fairbairn & Sykes 1987: 8):

	Police	Criminals
Killed	42	260
Wounded	100	193

Returning to Ireland, after the South's independence, a new police force was formed in the north following the model set by the RIC. The Royal Ulster Constabulary (RUC) was formed in 1922 after the division of the country, primarily along religious lines. Their situation in the 1920s was as desperate as that faced by their RIC predecessors; Catholic-versus-Protestant bloodshed continued for another decade. Then there was a long respite, with only sporadic – though sometimes severe – violence, until the late 1960s, when intense fighting again ripped through the land. From the 1920s the main counterinsurgency constables of the RUC were the 'B' Specials, units called to action in an emergency. From the 1920s the main counterinsurgency constables of the RUC were the 'B' Specials, units called to action in an emergency. These were local men who were trusted by many in the Protestant community, and who had their thumbs on the pulses of their neighbourhoods. Also, their ranks were filled with proficient marksmen, as shooting competitions were encouraged, and their weapon, until their disbandment in 1970, was the .455in Webley Mk VI. Historian Tim Pat Coogan proclaimed that 'The B Specials were the rock on which any mass movement by the IRA in the north has inevitably floundered [*sic*]'.

With the passing of the 'B' Specials of the RUC, so passed the .455in Webley from the front line after a long and impressive career. From the 1970s and through the 1980s, revolvers were increasingly becoming passé for law-enforcement applications. In America and in many other countries globally, revolvers continued to arm federal and urban law-enforcement agencies into the 1990s, when the use of semi-automatic pistols with large-capacity magazines finally became the norm.

What practical lessons for the defensive use of a handgun were learned during the fighting of World War I? Which of those principles taught in the musketry schools can still be applied by law-enforcement officers? World War I had been a catalyst for practical pistol fighting, in the guise of instinctive shooting, and these techniques were kept alive in the British Army and in law-enforcement agencies like the SMP. In World War II, Fairbairn, Sykes and an apprentice American officer (later Colonel) Rex Applegate instructed agents and elite soldiers in the art. Subsequently, the need for this type of instruction has never diminished.

Throughout the world today, in response to increased urban violent crime, drug trafficking and terrorist activities, countries have spawned legions of specialized paramilitary police units to deal with these problems. In the United States, SWAT teams exemplify this form of law enforcement; this acronym instantly conjures up mental images of elite officers, armed to the teeth, ready to win the day on the urban battlefield. Members of these teams are experts in house clearing, sniping, hostage rescue, man-tracking and many other extraordinary, high-risk feats required of them. Their methods of handgun training for close-quarters combat are not

In possibly one of the last-known official uses of Webley .455in revolvers, Sgt Donald Milliken of the Royal Ulster Constabulary issues a Mk VI revolver and .455in ammunition to a constable of the 'B' Specials before he goes on duty in Northern Ireland in August 1969. Kynoch halted production of their Mk VIZ cartridges that year, and the Mk VI was retired from RUC use in 1970. (Imperial War Museum HU 55870)

altogether disparate from those of the trench raiders of World War I. Although now the stance and the hold (two hands) on the pistol have changed somewhat, those basic tactical techniques still apply: grip the arm in the exact same manner whenever the weapon is drawn; draw and shoot with speed and accuracy without dwelling on the sight picture; keep your eyes on the threat; keep track of the number of rounds fired; perform a tactical reload whenever the magazine is more than half expended during a lull; take multiple shots at targets – 'double taps' at least; be able to clear a jam quickly at any moment; take advantage of cover; and offer a minimum profile through thresholds and while shooting around corners.

Even single-hand instinctive (point) shooting from various hip positions remains an effective way to engage an aggressor at minimum distances. These were fighting lessons learned the hard way nearly a century ago. Other training methods have been preserved as well. Realistic and complex courses of fire, including threat, non-threat and moving targets, and the use of various types of cover, are the accepted standard.

HOW HARD-HITTING WAS THE WEBLEY?

Much has been written on the power of the .455in round, and how its big bullet stopped aggressors in their tracks. However, looking at the ballistics of contemporary cartridges for a comparison, there is nothing inherently unique about the specifications of the Webley round. Muzzle energy is a very rough way of estimating the stopping power of a round; as the speed and the weight of a projectile increase, so should its destructiveness. Curiously, the muzzle energy of a .455in round wasn't appreciably different, and was in fact less, than similar loadings for its day.

So what gave the .455in its fame? Obviously, there are factors other than velocity and mass to consider when estimating the true defensive potential of a cartridge. In the era in which the contemporaries of the .455in Webley were developed, there was a maxim to which these cartridges all adhered: 'A little powder and a lot of lead, shoot them once and shoot them dead.' Therefore a heavy projectile moving at a moderate, subsonic (<1,126ft/sec), velocity was thought to be the perfect combination for a man-stopping load. Theoretically, with these characteristics, the bullet would strike its intended victim and expend all of its kinetic energy in the target. (It only takes 60ft/lb (81.35J) to knock a man over (Robinson 1940: 42) and *all* firearms cartridges, with the possible exception of the .22in short, have substantially more.) This was essentially true among large calibres loaded with soft lead bullets that would either expand or tumble inside the body; of course, a critical part of the anatomy would have to sustain the impact if optimal results were to be achieved. However, at some point increased velocity, even with a larger bullet – thus raising the kinetic energy of the cartridge – would have decreased dividends; the down-range effect of this combination would be dissipated by the tendency of the projectile to pass through tissue (without expanding or tumbling) and not dump its energy into it.[13] Also, it was thought then that mostly smaller higher-velocity, primarily jacketed, rounds were considerably less effective because of their tendency to over-penetrate.

	Bullet weight (grains)	Muzzle velocity (ft/sec)	Muzzle energy (ft/lb)
.455in Mk II	265	650	289
.45in Colt	255	960	500
.45in ACP	230	870	410
.44in Russian	246	750	310

[13] Today, high-velocity hollow-pointed bullets that expand on impact to expend their energy are loaded into handgun cartridges to circumvent the problem of over-penetration with increased velocity, but this solution would never have been considered in the early 20th century, simply due to the philosophy of the time.

The debate concerning the efficacy of these two categories of ammunition arose during the first decade of the 20th century, when the US Army was searching for a new service pistol, and has been argued ever since. Fighting during the Philippine Insurrection (1899–1902) had demonstrated that a light .38in round had been ineffectual against determined (and drug-crazed) Moro warriors. Older .45in Colt 1878 and 1873 revolvers were recalled as a stop-gap measure until something better could be found to arm the soldiers in the field. Shortly thereafter, the equivocal Thompson–LaGarde ammunition tests of 1904 on live cattle and carcasses (cattle and human) reaffirmed what was thought to be gospel at that time: small, fast-moving projectiles over-penetrated and didn't kill rapidly enough, whereas bullets of .45in or greater were optimal. These trials paved the way for the adoption first of the .45in ACP cartridge, then the Colt M1911 pistol. But generally, humans, with infrequent exceptions, bear little resemblance to cattle.

The SMP also performed its own (empirical) ammunition trials – though these were not veiled under the guise of a 'scientific' experiment, as the American tests had been – and their results are possibly more relevant in terms of real-world situations (Fairbairn & Sykes 1987: 72–80). The SMP's duty files contained literally thousands of records of encounters in which both constable and criminal had been shot, by an assortment of bullets of different calibres. Pros and cons for projectiles both great and small were observed and noted. Larger calibres were most effective when their bullets struck closer to the centre of the body; their mass was retained and the effect of their energy dump was most dramatic in the vital areas of the thorax and abdomen. Though penetration was still an issue in soft tissues, the lighter, fast-moving missiles – such as bullets from a 7.63mm Mauser – caused considerable damage through hydraulic shock in muscle, liquefying it (referred to as being 'pulped'), and since they

A still from the 1964 film *Zulu*, which depicts the 1879 battle defending the Rorke's Drift outpost in Natal. Note that the actor Stanley Baker is wielding a World War I-era Webley .455in Mk VI. (Diamond Films/The Kobal Collection)

had a greater tendency to fragment, especially when hitting bone, severe damage adjacent to the wound channel was common.

By and large, what was established by the SMP data supported the level of marksmanship for the .455 required by Capt Tracy during World War I: 'the ability to put a shot into a 16" × 12" rectangle', or the size of a human chest. The target area used presently in defensive handgun training is the same, though now referred to as the 'centre of mass'. The .455in round was a man-stopper, when used according to training, but so were other cartridges similar to it. The bottom line is that the efficacy of a cartridge, or a handgun, depends on the expertise of the user. Without sufficient training, even a weapon of great power is of little use. This ideal was what Tracy, Noel and others had tried to instil in their pupils so long ago, and cannot be argued against with any justification at present.

FILM: AN ARM THAT DEFIES TIME

In film, when a revolver's cylinder is flopped to one side for reloading (if it is ever reloaded in a film), what make of revolver is it? A Colt? A Smith & Wesson? But when a large hand-filling pistol is broken open (especially by a well-regarded British actor) for the same purpose, then it must be a Webley! Alright, yes, there have been recent pictures that have portrayed cow-pokes armed with Italian reproductions of the hinge-framed .45in S&W Schofield; however, when a 'typically English' revolver is needed on the silver screen, the .455in Webley Mk VI is usually the star. What is more amazing is that the Webley's cameo appearances have transcended time. Mk VIs were used anachronistically to arm British officers in *Zulu* and its prequel, *Zulu Dawn*, which depicted the 1879 battles at Rorke's Drift and Isandhlwana, respectively. Then when Charlton Heston, aka General Charles Gordon, lost his head at *Khartoum* in 1966 (or was it 1885?) to the soldiers of the Mahdi (Lawrence Olivier), the immortal revolver was again in the footlights.

Later depictions may not stretch the imagination quite as much. The Second Boer War epic *Breaker Morant* yet again depicts Harry Morant (Edward Woodward) and his fellow officers armed with square-butted Webleys. Even in America, where an amazing deposition of surplus .455s had taken place by the 1960s, depictions of earlier Prohibition-era gangsters armed with then current-issue British service revolvers in preference to Colts and S&Ws argues realism to an extreme. Actors Robert De Niro in *The Godfather Part II* and J.E. Freeman in *Miller's Crossing* exterminate their rivals with an arm that at the time depicted (1920s) was still in use defending the British Empire. Ultimately, a large and ominous handgun is just that, and whatever suitable item was available at the 'prop house' on the day of filming was utilized. Possibly more in tempo with the times, and in better agreement with history, blockbusters such as *Lawrence of Arabia*, *The Longest Day* and *Gallipoli* depict the weapon more realistically, since the depiction of events in these films fall well within the realm of the revolver's service career.

CONCLUSION

WHERE HAVE ALL THE WEBLEYS GONE?

The immediate post-World War II period for Britain was indeed a lean time. Food rationing lasted until 1954, and there was also the price of the war from which the country had to recuperate. To aid the country's depleted coffers, thousands of tons of Lee-Enfield rifles and Webley revolvers were exported to buyers overseas, fetching millions of pounds sterling. Rifles, machine guns, pistols and revolvers were sold by the pound, and not by the piece. A trade in wholesale weaponry abounded. America was a vast black hole for the purchase of these weapons due to that country's seemingly insatiable appetite for sporting guns. Golden State Arms in California, Val Forgett's Navy Arms in New Jersey and Sam Cumming's Interarms in Virginia were three of the largest recipients during this period. It may seem like a travesty now, but vintage Mausers and Enfields of all ages were cut to dimensions that more suited the hunter than the collector. Webleys also fell to the chop, since there was a dearth of .455in ammunition in the United States and – .45in ACP being as common as dirt – the breech ends of Webley cylinders were machined down to accept that All-American cartridge in half-moon clips. There is some evidence that cylinder throats and recoil shields of surplus .455in revolvers were also sometimes relieved to accept the greater length and thicker rims of the .45in Long Colt round.

What has happened to this motherlode of matériel over the decades typifies the rudiments of a free-market economy: when a commodity is plentiful, then it's cheap; conversely, when supply is bottlenecked, costs rise. In the late 1950s, even with the labour involved for their conversion to .45in ACP, good-quality early Webleys (pre-Mk VI) were sold for the

To provide space for either half-moon clips containing .45in ACP rounds, or individual Auto Rim cartridges, 0.0827in (2.10mm) has been shaved from the breech face of the right-hand cylinder. (Author)

princely sum of $15 ($115 today), and the highly desirable Mk VI for $29 ($223 today). Over the years the practicality of, as well as the demand for, converted revolvers has declined, whereas the desire among collectors to own an unadulterated piece of history has skyrocketed. Prices for excellent unmodified specimens of the first five marks – especially Mks I, II and III – are comfortably over $1,000, with Mk VIs in the upper hundreds, and Mk IVs and Mk Vs somewhere in-between. Service or commercial revolvers with provenance, with any sort of attribution to a specific unit or an individual, fetch an additional premium.

Importation laws for Webley revolvers (both the .455in and the .380in) were changed after the implementation of the Gun Control Act of 1968. Stringent rules on the safety characteristics of arms coming into the United States came into place. Specifically concerning Webleys, their rebounding safeties are now considered not robust enough to withstand a blow to the hammer without significant risk of a discharge. Importers keen on bringing these pistols into the country had to devise a hammer-blocking device suitable for the scrutiny of the Bureau of Alcohol, Tobacco and Firearms (BATF). In the 1970s and 1980s this was still economically feasible. Century Arms in Vermont imported hundreds of Webley Mk VIs during this period, fitting them all with an internal hammer block, evidenced only by the protrusion of a screw head on the right side of the frame. Though these revolvers were imported in their original calibre, which collectors at that time were beginning to appreciate, the addition of the safety did diminish their value.

In the UK today, the Webley's price presently more depends on the item as an icon rather than the arm's functionality. Exceedingly restrictive handgun laws (since 1997) have successfully suppressed the desire of most collectors to own a working modern collectable revolver or rifle, but the desire to own a historical artefact remains intact. Tons of historically significant arms of every description are currently being imported into the UK from ex-colonial nations like Zimbabwe, thankfully not for destruction but for deactivation. Though present deactivation specifications are strict, leaving the owner with nothing more than a solid-fused inactive piece of the past, they allow those who cherish history to own a part of it. There is still an opportunity in Britain for those willing enough to succumb to stringent government scrutiny to keep functioning 'heritage' (pre-1919), weapons at home without ammunition or at a shooting club with ammunition, where they may be enjoyed to their fullest. The market again decides the price; deactivated and neutered relics of the Empire in good condition sell on average from £450 to £600, whereas the fully functional equivalent may obtain only £250 at auction.

The .455in Webley is not a thing of the past, but is a weapon that competed successfully with every other challenging pistol type of its day and has contributed significantly to today's combat fighting methods. It was not just a good weapon, but an excellent one. Its action was a proven design and used subsequently by Colt and others; it was solid, the best that late 19th-century engineering could produce, a design which endured well into the 20th century. Furthermore, its extreme utility and prevalence on the battlefields of World War I, through the prescience of pragmatic and forward-thinking minds, allowed the .455in Webley to be one of the catalysts for the techniques that still aid the warriors of law enforcement today.

With loins sufficiently girded, Cdr A. Bloomer, a pilot with the Fleet Air Arm during the Korean War, would seem ready for any battle. Amongst his weapons are *khukri* and Fairbairn–Sykes fighting knives, four S&W .380in Victory Models, and a Webley .455in Mk VI in his boot. Not a man to trifle with. (Imperial War Museum MH 33600)

GLOSSARY

CYLINDER BOLT: A tooth protruding from the frame of a revolver that engages slots in the perifery of the cylinder to prevent arbitrary rotation. The function of a cylinder bolt may be incorporated with that of a cylinder stop, as on most current revolvers, or it may be located at a separate position on the frame – as on the .455in Webleys, where it is known as a trigger stop.

CYLINDER STOP: An indexing tooth extending up from the base of the frame to engage slots in the circumference of the cylinder. This tooth assists to 'stop' the cylinder's rotation precisely at the battery position (where the striker, chamber and barrel are all in the optimal linear alignment for firing).

DOUBLE-ACTION: The functions of (both) cocking the hammer (or striker) and releasing it, to discharge a firearm, through one long continuous pull of the trigger. Previously known as **trigger-action, trigger-cocking, or continuous action.**

EJECTOR ROD: A cylindrical device used for the extraction and ejection of cartridges from, primarily, early types of revolvers. Ejector rods were commonly found fitted either in a parallel arrangement with the barrel or separately, held captive or screwed into the base of the revolver's butt.

GROOVES: The helical channels in a rifled firearm's barrel.

HALF COCK: A safety notch in the breast (front) of a firearm's hammer, or on the cocking piece of a rifle, that engages the sear in a solid captive fashion at an intermediate position (between full cock and firing positions), preventing the discharge of the weapon if the trigger is inadvertantly pulled or the hammer is accidently struck.

HEADSPACE: The distance between the base of a cartridge case (case head) and the breech face or bolt of a modern firearm. Too much headspace might allow the case to rupture when fired, or the striker to be ineffectual in detonating the primer; too little won't allow the breech block, bolt, or revolver to close properly.

HINGE PIN: The pin securing the component parts of a hinge at their point of articulation, here specifically, the pivot point of the barrel and frame of a hinge-frame revolver. Also **joint pin.**

HINGE-FRAMED PISTOL: A revolver, or less commonly a semi-automatic pistol (e.g. Beretta M21 'Bobcat'), where the frame is articulated at a point allowing the barrel to be raised or lowered exposing its breech for loading or unloading.

LANDS: The prominent helical ridges in a rifled firearm's barrel.

LOADING GATE: The hinged plate found on the frames of many types of primitive revolvers covering the breech ends of their cylinders. When opened, access to the chambers is permitted for either loading or unloading metallic cartridges.

PAWL (HAND): The finger-like projection of the lockwork of a revolver which engages the rear face (ratchet) of the cylinder to rotate it into battery (firing) position.

PRIMER: 1. As a (priming) compound, it is a highly pressure-sensitive explosive, used in minute quantities, to ignite a cartridge's primary charge of propellant. 2. As a component part of a centre-fire cartridge, it is a cup-shaped reservoir of thin metal containing a priming compound; placed centrally at the base of the cartridge, it is struck by the hammer nose, firing pin, etc. to ignite the round's propellant during discharge.

RECOIL SHIELD: This is the [roughly] circular plate of metal behind the cylinder of a revolver that protects the firer from the hazards of a ruptured cartridge and through which the hammer nose protudes to fire a round.

SINGLE-ACTION: The hammer is cocked independently from any function of the trigger mechanism; the function of the trigger is used solely for releasing the hammer and discharging the firearm. Previously known as **single practice**

STACKING: A progressive stiffening felt during pull-through on a double-action trigger.

TIP-UP: Referring here to a type of hinge-framed pistol (see above) with the pivot point for the hinge at the top front edge of the frame, so when the barrel is released it rotates, or 'tips up' over the frame, to expose its breech-end.

BIBLIOGRAPHY

PRIMARY SOURCES

List of Changes paragraphs
LoC §1738, 26 November 1868
LoC §1739, 21 December 1868
LoC §2450, 24 December 1872
LoC §6844, 29 July 1891 and 26 September 1892
LoC §7687, 23 August 1894
LoC §7816, 1 October 1894
LoC §9039, 5 October 1897
LoC §9159, 21 July 1897
LoC §9787, 21 July 1899
LoC §16783, 9 December 1913
LoC §17319, 5 and 24 May 1915
LoC §18980, 1917
LoC §23958, 9 February 1921
LoC §A1636, 1926
LoC §A6862, 31 July 1932
LoC §B3313, March 1940
LoC §B5974, April 1942

Small Arms Committee minutes
SAC Minute 248, *Suggested Two-Piece Hammer For Revolvers*,
    31 March 1920
SAC Minute 265, *Revolver Dummy Cartridge*, 22 June 1920
SAC Minute 428, *Revolver Pistol, .38-Inch, Submitted By Messrs.
    Webley & Scott, Ltd.*, 30 November 1921
SAC Minute 462, *Pistol, Webley, Mark VI. Report On*, 26 April 1922
SAC Minute 474, *Webley & Scott, Ltd. .455-Inch Revolver Converted
    To Take .22-Inch Ammunition*, 24 May 1922
SAC Minute 516, *Application For Adapter Tube To Fire .22
    Ammunition From Service Pistol – Report On The Trial Of The
    .22 Adapter Tube*, 20 December 1922
SAC Minute 518, *Pistol, Webley, Mark VI. Report On*, 20 December 1922
SAC Minute 560, *Application For Adapter Tube To Fire .22-Inch
    Ammunition From Service Pistol – Report By Chief Instructor,
    Light Automatic Wing, Small Arms School, On .22-Inch Adapter
    Tubes And 6-Shot Cylinders. Details Of Trials Of .22-Inch
    Revolver, Adapter Tubes And 6-Shot Cylinder*, 17 October 1923
SAC Minute 683, *Adapter Tube To Fire .22-Inch Ammunition From
    Service Pistol*, 29 July 1925
SAC Minute 862, *Pistols, Revolver, .455-Inch, Mk. VI, Converted To
    Fire .22-Inch Ammunition*, 23 November 1927
SAC Minute 1291, *Pistol Revolver 0.38-Inch, Proposed Trial Of
    Samples Taken From Run Of Work*, 12 April 1933

SAC Minute 1647, *Automatic Pistol By Société Alsacienne De Constructions Mécaniques*, 10 March 1937

SAC Minute 1660, *Automatic Pistol By Société Alsacienne De Constructions Mécaniques – Proposed Purchase Of A Sample*, 2 June 1937

Ordnance Committee memoranda

OC 85, *Pistols. Revolver, 0.38. Modification*, 5 June 1938

Ordnance Board memoranda

OB 255, *Pistols. Revolver, 0.38 inch. Design for manufacture*, 20 January 1939

OB 645, *Pistols. Revolver, 0.38 inch. Design for manufacture*, 24 February 1939

SECONDARY SOURCES

Anonymous (1983). *Tank Corps Roll of Honour*. Birmingham: Midland Medals (originally London: HMSO, 1919).

Bester, R., et al. (2003). *Small Arms of the Anglo-Boer War 1899–1902*. Brandfort: Kraal Publishers.

Bickers, R. (2004). *Empire Made Me: An Englishman Adrift In Shanghai*. London: Penguin Books.

Bruce, G. (1992). *Webley & Scott Automatic Pistols*. Dietikon, Zürich: Stocker-Schmid Publishing Company.

Chamberlain, W.H.J. and A.W.F. Taylerson (1976). *Adams Revolvers*. London: Barrie and Jenkins.

Chamberlain, W.H.J. and A.W.F. Taylerson (1989). *Revolvers of the British Services, 1854–1954*. Bloomfield and Alexandra Bay, NY: Museum Restoration Service.

Churchill, W.S. (1899). *The River War: An Historical Account of The Reconquest of the Soudan*, 2 vols. London: Longmans, Green. Available from http://www.fordham.edu/Halsall/mod/1898churchill-omdurman.asp (accessed 13 December 2011).

Coogan, Tim Pat, *The I.R.A.* New York, NY: HarperCollins. (p.37).

Cuthbertson, S. (1999). *Worldwide Webley and the Harrington and Richardson Connection*. Gabriols: Ballista Publishing.

Fairbairn, Capt W.E. and Capt E.A. Sykes (1987). *Shooting To Live*. Boulder, CO: Paladin Press (originally 1942).

Graves, R. (1998). *Goodbye to All That*. New York, NY: Doubleday.

HBSA (1990). J.B. Fenby, letter to the editor, *Shooting* magazine, 24 October 1888. Reprinted in *The Journal of the Historical Breechloading Smallarms Association*, Vol. 2 (3), 2.

Labbett, P. (1993). *British Small Arms Ammunition 1864–1938 (Other Than .303 Inch Calibre)*. London: P. Labbett.

Milner, R. (2008). 'House of Webley – Gunmakers'. A lecture presented to members of the Historical Breechloading Shooters Association on their 35th Anniversary in August 2008.

Noel, J.B.L., (1918). *How To Shoot With A Revolver*, London: Foster

Groom & Co.

Pegler, Martin (1993). 'The Pritchard–Greener Bayonet', *Journal of the Arms and Armour Society*, Vol. 14 (3), 163–73.

Quinn, T. (1993). *Tales of the Old Soldiers*. Stroud: Alan Sutton.

Rawling, B. (1992). *Surviving Trench Warfare: Technology and the Canadian Corps, 1914–1918*, Toronto, Buffalo, NY, and London: University of Toronto Press.

Robinson, Capt E.H. (1940). *The Pistol In War – Training With Revolver And Self-Loading Pistol*. Aldershot: Gale & Polden, Ltd.

Skennerton, I. (1988). *British Small Arms of World War 2 (The Complete Reference Guide to Weapons, Makers' Codes & 1936– 1946 Contracts)*. Margate, Queensland: Ian D. Skennerton.

Taylerson, A.W.F. (1966). *The Revolver 1865–1888*. New York, NY: Bonanza Books–Crown Publishers, Inc.

Taylerson, A.W.F. (1994). 'One of Our Drivers Shot Himself Through the Foot…', *Classic Arms and Militaria*, Vol. 1, No. 2. Droitwich: Peterson Publications Ltd, 18–21.

Thomas, D. (2010). 'The Pistol in British Military Service during the Great War'. Unpublished master's dissertation (SRN 592736), University of Birmingham.

Tracy, Capt C.D. (1916). *Revolver Shooting In War – A Practical Handbook*. London: Sifton Praed.

Tracy, Capt C.D. (1918). *The Service Revolver and How to Use It*. London: Harrison and Sons Ltd.

War Office (1898). *The Musketry Regulations*. London: HMSO.

War Office (1907a). *Manual of Military Law*, 5th ed. London: HMSO.

War Office (1907b). [Naval] *Musketry Regulations*. London: HMSO.

War Office (1909). [Army] *Musketry Regulations*. London: HMSO.

War Office (1910). [Army] *Musketry Regulations*. London: HMSO.

War Office (1911). [Army] *Musketry Regulations*. London: HMSO.

War Office (1912). [Army] *Musketry Regulations*. London: HMSO.

War Office (1913). [Army] *Musketry Regulations*. London: HMSO.

War Office (1914). [Army] *Musketry Regulations*. London: HMSO.

War Office (1924). *Small Arms Training*, Vol. II. London: HMSO.

War Office (1931a). *Instructions for Armourers*. London: HMSO.

War Office (1931b). *Small Arms Training*, Vols I–V. London: HMSO.

War Office (1932). Annual Revolver Course (Appendix III to Vol. IV). London: HMSO.

War Office (1937). *Instructions for Armourers*. London: HMSO.

War Office (1941). *Small Arms Training*, Vol. 1, Pamphlet No. 11, 'Pistol (.455 in.) 1937'. Reprinted under authority of HMSO for General Staff, NZ Military Forces. Wellington: E.V. Paul.

War Office (1942). *Small Arms Training*, Vol. 1, Pamphlet No. 11, 'Pistol (.38-inch)', London: HMSO.

Winans, W. (1904). *Hints on Revolver Shooting*. London and New York, NY: G.P. Putnam's Sons.

INDEX